Fresh food cooking with
Dairy Foods

R&R PUBLISHING PTY LTD

CONTENTS

Introduction

Dairy Foods – 'Cool' Snack Food and 'Essential' Ingredient

I am delighted to be given this opportunity to write an Introduction on the dietary value of dairy products in today's lifestyle. Working as a clinical dietitian on the geriatric ward of a busy city hospital, I wish to stress a nutritional issue about which I have come to feel very strongly. All too often I have been confronted with patients suffering from fractured bones. Much of this suffering could have been prevented by an adequate intake of dairy foods throughout life, combined with a healthy lifestyle. An estimated 56 per cent of women over the age of sixty years, and 29 per cent of men of this age, suffer from osteoporosis-related fractures.

Dairy foods include all milk products obtained from domesticated mammals such as cows, sheep, goats, water-buffaloes and camels. These products include milk, cheese, yogurt, ice cream, butter and cream. You will find a chapter devoted to each of these dairy foods in 'Fresh Food Cooking with Dairy Foods'. In addition to the delicious recipes, you will find that each chapter provides useful information on the method of manufacture, varieties, and nutritional value of dairy products.

Nutrition professionals encourage the inclusion of dairy foods in the diet predominantly due to their excellent calcium content. It is estimated that approximately 65 per cent of calcium in the western diet is obtained from milk and milk products. Dairy foods also supply phosphorus, protein and B-complex vitamins (especially riboflavin), as well as moderate amounts of potassium, magnesium and zinc.

Calcium is a mineral which is required by the body to build strong bones and teeth. Additional important functions of calcium include healthy nerve and muscle activity, and its role in clotting the blood, which is necessary after a skin cut or abrasion.

The recommended intake for calcium is dependent upon age, with the recommended daily intake (RDI) reflecting changes in the body with age. The table (right) gives the current Australian National Health and Medical Research Council (NH&MRC) recommendations for daily calcium intake.

Australian National Health and Medical Research Council (NH&MRC) Calcium Recommended Daily Intake (RDI)

Stage of Life	Sex	Age	RDI (mg/day)
Infants (Up to 12 months)	Male & Female	0–6 months • breast fed	300
		0–6 months • bottle fed	500
		7–12 months	550
Young Children (7 years and under)	Male & Female	1–3 years	700
		4–7 years	800
Older Children (8 years and older)	Male	8–11 years	800
		12–15 years	1200
		16–18 years	1000
	Female	8–11 years	900
		12–15 years	1000
		16–18 years	800
Adults	Male	19–64 years	800
		64+ years	800
	Female	19–54 years	800
		• Pregnancy	add 300
		• Lactation	add 400
		54+ years	1000

It will be observed from the above table that an increased daily calcium intake is recommended: (i) during the growth period of teenage years (for both males and females); (ii) for women over 54 years; and (iii) for pregnant and lactating women.

In the case of women aged over 54 years, the recommended higher intake is based on the need for greater calcium intake after menstruation ceases (referred to as 'menopause'). After the menopause, less oestrogen (a female reproductive hormone) is produced, resulting in an increased loss of calcium from the bones. If more dietary calcium is not consumed, osteoporosis (a decline in bone density) may occur.

To assist in maintaining bone density, pregnant and lactating women must take extra care to ensure adequate calcium intake. During pregnancy, the growing foetus means that an extra serve of calcium is required by the woman, and during lactation the demands of the suckling infant require a higher calcium intake by the mother.

Therefore, the exact number of serves of dairy foods required each day will vary according to an individual's calcium requirements. However, in general, dietitians recommend three serves of dairy foods each day for bone health. Each serve provides approximately 300mg of calcium and is equivalent to the following: a 250mL glass of milk (whole milk/reduced-fat/skimmed), a 40g block of cheddar cheese (natural/reduced-fat), 400g of cottage cheese, 150g of ricotta cheese, or a 200g tub of yogurt (natural/reduced-fat).

A product which is often used to replace dairy foods is soy beverage, and its associated products. Soy beverage (extracted from soy beans) is useful in the diets of those who choose not to drink milk, perhaps due to a dislike of the taste of milk, or because of lactose intolerance. Although soy beverage does not contain lactose (a sugar found in milk), it is a controversial source of calcium.

There are products available which can be used to breakdown the lactose in milk before it is digested. These enable milk (and milk products) to be included in the diet of a lactose-intolerant individual. One common product is 'Lactaid' drops and tablets. However, studies have shown that most people with lactose intolerance can still tolerate up to 10–14g of lactose without any symptoms. This is the amount present in 200–300mL of whole milk (an average glass). A person with lactose intolerance should ask a dietitian or doctor for more information.

Of concern to dietitians is the common observation that girls and women often avoid dairy foods in an effort to lose weight. Today, however, there are many low fat and skim milks (and milk products) from which to choose. These enable females to have an adequate calcium intake, but without putting on weight. If you are watching your weight, substitute reduced fat/skim milk (and milk products) for the full fat version in the recipes in this book.

There is no doubt that the best source of calcium for good bone health is dairy foods. However, there may be some cases which warrant the need for a calcium supplement, as prescribed by your doctor. The ability of bones to absorb calcium from the supplement form is still unclear. It is therefore recommended that the minimum three serves of dairy foods per day be consumed, in conjunction with calcium supplements.

There are some foods which have been shown to decrease calcium absorption. Foods with a high phosphorus content should be avoided, such as cola drinks and cured meats (e.g. frankfurts). Bran and bran cereals (due to their phytic acid content), and some fruit and vegetables which contain oxalic acid (e.g. spinach) can also reduce calcium absorption, but these are of concern only if eaten in excessive amounts. A high fat intake, caffeine, and smoking, all reduce the amount of calcium absorbed by bones.

Exercise, however, has been shown to increase calcium absorption. It may take any form including, dancing, walking, gardening, swimming, tennis or aqua-aerobics (to name but a few). When choosing an activity for exercise, remember to choose those which you enjoy. This will help to ensure that you adhere to exercise for the recommended three times a week (for at least 20–30 minutes each time). Gradually work up from this recommendation if you can, allowing your body to gain the many other benefits of exercise (in addition to the benefit of increased calcium absorption by bones).

It may seem strange for a dietitian to be singing the praises of a cookbook which contains chapters on butter and cream. However, as all dietitians would agree, there is a place for such dairy foods in a healthy, balanced diet. The key to avoiding or controlling health problems (such as being overweight and/or the development of coronary heart disease), is to use such dairy products sparingly. When consuming recipes which feature butter and/or cream from 'Fresh Food Cooking with Dairy Foods', remember that a single portion is best!

Clearly, it is evident that a healthy, balanced diet, which includes a minimum of three serves of dairy food each day, combined with regular exercise (especially early in life), will assist in preventing future health problems, particularly fractured bones. As a female dietitian, in my late 20's, I would urge you to include more dairy foods in your (and your family's) diet, either as a 'cool' snack food, or as an 'essential' ingredient. 'Fresh Food Cooking with Dairy Foods' is the perfect reference to assist you in doing this... for your 'bones' sake'!

Happy, Healthy Cooking!

Carolyn Kelly
Consultant Dietitian

Milk

Cow's milk is the most complete of all foods, containing nearly all of the important nutritional constituents

The following table shows the composition of milk and why it is so good for you:

MILK

Lactose	Fats	Protein	Minerals	Calcium	Vitamins
The natural sugar in milk necessary for energy	The cream in milk which provides much of the necessary energy we require for normal daily activities	Essential for building body cells and for skin, hair and muscle growth	(e.g. phosphorus, magnesium and zinc); essential for general good health	Calcium and phosphorus help build strong bones and teeth	Strongest in B Group—Riboflavin, Thiamine, Niacin—which helps convert food to energy

Who should drink milk?

Everybody should drink milk! Milk is a complete food, and is also extremely good value.

Groups who benefit most are infants, children, teenagers, pregnant women, nursing mothers and post-menopausal women.

Milk can be consumed in a variety of ways. As a straight drink, ice-cold, it is deliciously refreshing and is almost a meal in itself. Mixed with fruit, ice cream, yogurt, nuts and other goodies, it becomes a super-shake—see the recipes in the milk chapter for ideas.

And, of course, it is used extensively in cooking, as you will see from the wide range of dishes in this cookbook.

	Regular	Extra Cream	Reduced Fat	Skim
Milk Fat	3.8%	4.8%	1.5%	0.1%
Protein	3.3%	3.3%	3.9%	3.4%
Milk Lactose	4.6%	4.6%	5.3%	4.7%
Calcium (mg per 100 mL)	118	118	145	129
Kilojoules (per 100 mL)	278	317	214	142
Calories (per 100 mL)	66	76	51	34

Osteoporosis

Osteoporosis is a complex condition which affects one in two women (and one in three men) over the age of 60 in Australia. As a result of a process called demineralisation, calcium is lost from the bones which become thin and brittle and liable to break easily.

In severe cases of osteoporosis, fractures can occur following slight knocks or as a result of the normal activities of daily living, such as lifting and bending.

There is no cure for osteoporosis.

Although there is no cure for osteoporosis, we can help to delay the onset of the disease by ensuring that all possible risks are minimised. An adequate intake of calcium throughout all stages of life, and regular weight-bearing exercise (for example, walking), are a great start.

Calcium is needed for building and maintaining bone mass. Everyone benefits from having more calcium in their diet.

Dairy products are an ideal source of calcium, as well as containing a variety of other important nutrients needed for a healthy, balanced diet.

Three glasses (each 250mL) of milk per day will provide sufficient calcium (900mg) for the average adult. This may be consumed over cereal, in cooking, in beverages or as a pure milk drink.

Longlife Milk

Longlife or UHT (ultra heat treated) milk is pure whole milk which has been ultra heat treated and packed under sterile conditions.

The special pack seals in the goodness, so the milk stays fresh without refrigeration for months (although refrigeration is required once the pack has been opened). Nothing is added—no chemicals and no preservatives.

Both fresh milk and Longlife milk can be used in all of the recipes using milk in this cookbook.

Poppy Seed and Carrot Damper Twists

Ingredients
2 cups self-raising flour
2 cups self-raising wholemeal flour
¾ cup MILK POWDER
¼ cup poppy seeds
1 carrot (grated)
2 spring onions (chopped)
1½ cups water
extra poppy seeds (for sprinkling)

Makes 12

Method

1. Sift flours and milk powder together. Mix in poppy seeds, carrot and spring onions.
2. Make a well in the centre, add water, and combine to form a soft dough. Knead lightly on a floured board until smooth. Divide into 24 pieces.
3. Twist 2 portions of dough together into sticks. Place on a baking tray lined with GLAD Bake and sprinkle with extra poppy seeds.
4. Bake (at 220°C) for 15 minutes. Serve as an accompaniment to soup.

Hint: To divide into 24 equal portions, first divide into 3 equal portions, then halve each portion (to gain 6 portions), halve again (now 12 portions) and once more (to make 24 portions).

Sweetcorn Pancakes with Avocado and Ham

Sweetcorn Pancakes with Avocado and Ham

(photographed above)

Ingredients

2 cups self-raising flour
3 eggs (lightly beaten)
1¾ cups MILK
1 x 130g can creamed corn
BUTTER (as required)
¼ cup LIGHT SOUR CREAM
¼ cup mayonnaise
¼ cup chives (snipped)
1 large avocado (sliced)
12 slices smoked ham

Method

1. Make a well in the centre of the flour and whisk into the well the eggs, milk and corn (to form a batter).
2. Lightly coat a crêpe pan with butter and heat. Pour in ¼ cup mixture and cook over medium heat (until bubbles appear on the surface and the underside is golden brown). Turn over and cook until golden.
3. Remove and keep warm. Continue with remaining mixture, buttering when necessary, to make 10–12 pancakes. Combine sour cream, mayonnaise and chives.
4. Wrap slices of avocado in ham and serve on top of pancakes with a dollop of sour cream mixture.

Serves 6

Ham and Cheese Soufflé

Ingredients

50g BUTTER
½ cup flour
½ teaspoon mustard
1¾ cups MILK
1 cup ham (finely chopped)
¾ cup TASTY CHEESE (grated)
black pepper (to taste)
4 eggs (separated)

Method

1. Preheat oven (to 190°C). Lightly butter a 6-cup soufflé dish.
2. Melt butter. Stir in flour and mustard, and cook for 1 minute. Add milk. Cook until sauce boils and thickens.
3. Remove from heat, add ham and cheese, and beat until cheese melts. Season to taste with pepper. Add beaten egg yolks.
4. Beat all 4 egg whites until stiff. Fold into sauce mixture.
5. Pour into soufflé dish. Bake (at 190°C) for 20–30 minutes (or until puffed and golden).

Serves 6

Jan's Handy Tip

If extra pancakes are prepared, and not immediately used, interleave with GLAD Go-Between, and then freeze for later use.

Cream of Oyster Soup

Ingredients

45g BUTTER
3 tablespoons flour
600mL fish stock
300mL MILK
lemon juice
anchovy essence
1 dozen oysters (fresh if available)

Method

1. Melt butter in a saucepan, add flour, and blend well without browning. Add stock, and stir (until boiling). Cook for 2 minutes.
2. Add milk and re-heat. Flavour with lemon juice and anchovy essence.
3. Blanch oysters (by pouring boiling water over them in a strainer) before adding to soup. Use this liquid as stock.
4. Add oysters just before serving.

Serves 6

Sweet Potato and Leek Soup

(photographed below)

Ingredients

20g BUTTER
1 leek (sliced)
500g orange sweet potato* (peeled and diced)
1 bay leaf
2 cups chicken stock
2 cups MILK
spring onion (for garnish)

Method

1. Melt the butter in a large saucepan, and cook leek (until softened).
2. Add sweet potato, bay leaf and stock, and cook (covered) for 15–20 minutes (or until vegetables are tender). Remove the bay leaf.
3. Purée until smooth. Pour the soup back into the saucepan, add the milk, and allow to heat through. Serve garnished with spring onion strips.

*Orange sweet potato is also known as kumera.

Serves 6

Sweet Potato and Leek Soup

Pumpkin Ricotta Bake

(photographed below)

Ingredients

400g butternut pumpkin (peeled and chopped)
2 rashers lean bacon (chopped)
4 spring onions (chopped)
2 eggs
1 cup reduced fat MILK
1 x 250g tub RICOTTA or COTTAGE CHEESE
¼ cup PARMESAN CHEESE (grated)
¼ cup bread crumbs (dried)
paprika (for sprinkling)

Method

1. Steam or microwave pumpkin (until tender), and place in an ovenproof dish or GLAD TuckAway Foil Tray.
2. Sauté bacon and spring onions in a non-stick pan (until cooked) and sprinkle over pumpkin.
3. Whisk together the eggs, milk and Ricotta cheese, and pour over pumpkin. Sprinkle with Parmesan, breadcrumbs and paprika.
4. Bake (at 200°C) for 30 minutes (until golden brown and set). Serve cut into wedges.

Serves 6

Vegetable Pasta

Ingredients

1 teaspoon BUTTER
2 cloves garlic
2 onions (chopped)
1 red capsicum (chopped)
1 green capsicum (chopped)
1 x 310g can sweet corn (drained
1 teaspoon oregano
black pepper (to taste)
1½ cups SKIM MILK
3 tablespoons flour
200g green fettucine (cooked to packet directions)

Method

1. Melt butter, and add garlic, onions and capsicums. Cook over gentle heat (until vegetables are soft).
2. Add corn, and season to taste with oregano and black pepper. Heat through.
3. Combine skim milk with flour. Add to pan, and stir (until sauce boils and thickens). Toss through hot pasta.

Serves 4–6

Pumpkin Ricotta Bake

Creamy Seafood Ragout

Creamy Seafood Ragout

(photographed above)

Ingredients

50g BUTTER
1 onion (chopped)
1 red capsicum (chopped)
1 stalk celery (sliced)
2 tablespoons plain flour
2 cups MILK
½ cup dry white wine
1 tablespoon French mustard
½ cup CHEDDAR CHEESE (grated)
250g scallops (debearded)
250g green prawns (shelled)
250g white fish fillets (cubed)
1 x 190g can champignons (drained)
cooked rice (for serving)

Method

1. Melt the butter in a saucepan and sauté the onion, capsicum and celery (until softened). Add the flour and cook, stirring, for 1 minute.
2. Add the milk, wine and mustard, and cook (until thickened).
3. Add the remaining ingredients and simmer for 5 minutes (until the seafood is just cooked). Serve with rice.

Serves 6

Salmon Mousse

Ingredients

300mL reduced fat MILK
100g creamed COTTAGE CHEESE
1 celery stalk
¼ small onion
1 teaspoon lemon rind (grated)
½ teaspoon dill (weed)
¼ teaspoon tarragon leaves
1 tablespoon gelatine
¼ cup water
1 x 220g can red salmon (drained and bones removed)

Method

1. Process milk, creamed cottage cheese, celery, onion, lemon rind and herbs in a blender. Transfer to a bowl.
2. Soften gelatine in water. Place over hot water until dissolved.
3. Blend gelatine and salmon into milk mixture. Pour into a 2-cup tureen. Chill until set.
4. Serve as an appetiser with crisp vegetables (such as sliced aniseed, blanched).

Makes 2 cups

Jan's Handy Tip

Always wash fish (and dry with paper towels) before placing it in refrigerator. It is best to wrap fish with OSO Aluminium Foil, rather than plastic film (which makes fish sweat).

Multi-Pancakes

Pancakes

Ingredients

1 egg
300mL MILK
1 cup sifted flour

Method

1. Beat eggs and milk. Beat in flour. Stand for 30 minutes. Beat again.
2. Heat a non-stick frypan. Pour in approximately ¼ cup of mixture to make a 20cm pancake.
3. Cook over medium heat (until golden on underside).
4. Flip over and cook other side.

Makes 6 Pancakes

Basic Béchamel Sauce

Ingredients

750mL MILK
1 onion (roughly chopped)
2 bay leaves
6 black peppercorns
60g BUTTER
6 tablespoons flour

Method

1. Combine milk, onion, bay leaves and peppercorns. Bring to the boil, then cool and strain.
2. Melt butter, add flour, and cook for 1 minute.
3. Add milk, and stir (until sauce boils and thickens).
4. Use as a base for one of the variations listed (each of which fills and sauces 6 pancakes).

Béchamel Sauce Variations

1. Mushroom and White Wine Sauce

Ingredients

1 teaspoon BUTTER
300g mushrooms (sliced)
½ cup white wine

Method

1. Melt butter, and sauté mushrooms. Add to béchamel. Spoon 2–3 tablespoons onto each pancake, and roll up. Place in ovenproof dish, cover, and heat for 20–30 minutes (at 180°C).
2. Add wine to remaining sauce, and stir over heat (until smooth and heated through). Serve over pancakes.

2. Mustardy Ham and Cheese Sauce

Ingredients

6 slices leg ham
2 tablespoons PARMESAN CHEESE (grated)
½ cup TASTY CHEDDAR CHEESE (grated)
¼–½ teaspoon dry mustard
½ cup MILK (extra)

Method

1. Cut ham into strips. Scatter over surface of pancakes.
2. Add cheese and mustard to hot sauce, and beat (until cheese melts).
3. Place 2–3 tablespoons onto each pancake, and roll up. Place in ovenproof dish, cover and heat for 20–30 minutes (at 180°C).
4. Add extra milk to remaining sauce, and stir over heat (until smooth and heated through). Serve over pancakes.

Basic Custard Sauce

Ingredients

3 cups MILK
2 tablespoons custard powder
2 tablespoons cornflour
2 tablespoons caster sugar

Method

1. Combine ½ cup of the milk with the custard powder, cornflour and sugar to make a smooth paste.
2. Bring remaining milk to the boil, and pour onto custard mixture. Stir briskly (until thick and smooth).
3. Use as a base for one of the sweet variations listed (each of which fills 6 pancakes).

Custard Sauce Variations

1. Orange Apricot Pancakes

Ingredients

½ cup apricots (chopped and dried)
2 tablespoons dark rum
2 tablespoons orange juice
1 x 825g can apricots (drained)

Method

1. Soak apricots in rum and orange juice overnight. Add to basic custard sauce.
2. Divide apricots between pancakes and sprinkle with extra rum (if desired). Top with 1–2 tablespoons of custard.
3. Fold each in half, and then in half again (to form a cone shape). Place in an ovenproof dish, cover and heat through (at 180°C) for 20–30 minutes. Serve with hot orange apricot custard.

2. Butterscotch Banana Pancakes

Ingredients

60g UNSALTED BUTTER
4 tablespoons brown sugar
2 tablespoons honey
4 large bananas
2 tablespoons brandy

Method

1. In a heavy-based frying pan, combine the butter, brown sugar and honey, and cook (until sugar melts and froths). Add thickly sliced bananas to caramel. Remove from heat.
2. Divide bananas among pancakes.
3. To make Brandy Butterscotch Custard, add any remaining caramel and brandy to basic custard. Place 1–2 tablespoonfuls of custard onto each pancake.
4. Fold in half, and then in half again (to form a cone shape). Place in an ovenproof dish. Cover and heat through (at 180°C) for 20–30 minutes. Serve with remaining hot Brandy Butterscotch Custard.

H
min
PROG

Harlequin Chowder

(photographed below)

Ingredients

50g BUTTER
½ red capsicum (diced)
1 onion (diced)
2 tablespoons flour
4 cups MILK
¼ cup SKIM MILK POWDER
2 cups chicken stock
1 large potato (peeled and diced)
440g can creamed corn
½ cup frozen peas (thawed)
½ cup REDUCED FAT CHEDDAR CHEESE
crusty bread (for serving)

Method

1. Melt the butter in a saucepan, add the capsicum, and sauté the onion (until softened). Add the flour and cook (stirring) for 1 minute.
2. Add the combined milk and milkpowder, and the stock, and stir (until slightly thickened).
3. Add the potato and corn, and simmer for 10 minutes (or until the potatoes are tender). Add the peas and cheese, and simmer for a further 5 minutes. Serve with crusty bread.

Serves 4

Chicken Macaroni Cheese

Ingredients

25g BUTTER
1 onion (diced)
2 rashers bacon (sliced)
2 tablespoon plain flour
2½ cups MILK
2 tablespoons tomato paste
500g spiral pasta (cooked)
2 cups chicken (cooked)
1 cup CHEDDAR CHEESE (grated)
2 zucchini (sliced and blanched)
1 tomato (chopped)
¼ cup PARMESAN or ROMANO CHEESE (grated)

Method

1. Melt the butter in a saucepan, and sauté the onion and bacon. Add the flour, and cook for 2 minutes. Add milk and tomato paste, and stir (until thickened).
2. Combine the pasta, chicken, cheddar cheese, zucchini and tomato, and place in an ovenproof dish or GLAD TuckAway Foil Tray.
3. Pour the sauce over the above, and top with Parmesan cheese. Bake (at 180°C) for 20–25 minutes.

Serves 8

Harlequin Chowder

Creamy Tuna and Mushroom Risotto

Creamy Tuna and Mushroom Risotto

(photographed above)

Ingredients

2 cups water
2 chicken stock cubes (crumbled)
3 cups MILK
30g BUTTER
1 leek (finely sliced)
300g button mushrooms (sliced)
¼ cup parsley (chopped)
1 cup short grain rice
1 x 210g can tuna (drained)
½ cup PARMESAN CHEESE
salt and pepper (to taste)

Method

1. Heat the water in a large saucepan. Add the crumbled stock cubes, and heat until dissolved. Add the milk, and bring to simmering point.
2. Melt the butter in a large saucepan, and sauté the leek and mushrooms (until softened). Add parsley and rice, and cook (stirring continuously) for 1 minute.
3. Add ½ cup of the simmering milk mixture and cook while stirring (until the liquid is absorbed). Continue to add the milk, ½ cup at a time, cooking until liquid is absorbed before adding more liquid.
4. The rice should now be creamy (but still 'al dente'). Stir in the tuna and Parmesan cheese, season to taste, and allow to heat through before serving.

Serves 4

Sesame Chicken Curry

Ingredients

20g BUTTER
1 onion (chopped)
4 chicken fillets (skinned and cut into strips)
1 tablespoon curry powder
1 stalk celery (sliced)
1 zucchini (sliced)
1 apple (chopped)
1 cup NATURAL YOGURT
2 tablespoons SKIM MILK POWDER
1 tablespoon cornflour
¾ cup REDUCED FAT CHEDDAR CHEESE (grated)
½ cup dried apricots (chopped)
2 tablespoons sesame seeds (toasted)
rice (for serving)

Method

1. Melt the butter in a frying pan, and sauté the onion, chicken and curry powder (for 5 minutes).
2. Add the celery, zucchini and apple, and cook for 2 minutes (or until softened).
3. Combine the yogurt, milk powder, cornflour, cheese and apricots, and add to the pan, stirring without boiling (until heated through).
4. Sprinkle with toasted sesame seeds, and serve with rice.

Serves 4

Jan's Handy Tip

Place leftovers in GLAD TuckAways and keep in freezer. Make sure that you note the ingredients and date on top.

Mini Banana Puddings with Passionfruit Custard

Mini Banana Puddings with Passionfruit Custard

(photographed above)

Ingredients

50g BUTTER
⅓ cup caster sugar
rind of 1 lemon (grated)
1 egg (lightly beaten)
½ cup SKIM MILK
1 cup self-raising flour
1 banana (mashed)
1 tablespoon custard powder
2 tablespoons caster sugar (extra)
1 cup SKIM MILK (extra)
⅓ cup passionfruit pulp

Method

1. Cream the butter, sugar and lemon rind (until light and fluffy). Add the egg, milk, flour and banana.
2. Pour into 6 buttered and lined ½-cup timbale moulds. Place into a baking dish filled with 2cm of hot water. Bake uncovered (at 180°C) for 30 minutes. Stand for 5 minutes before turning out.
3. To make custard, blend custard powder and extra sugar with a small amount of extra milk in a saucepan. Add remaining milk and passionfruit and heat, stirring continuously (until thickened).
4. Serve hot puddings with passionfruit custard.

Serves 6

Peach Crunch

Ingredients

2 cups self-raising flour
½ cup caster sugar
1 x 800g can peach halves (in syrup)
¾ cup MILK
1 egg
40g BUTTER (melted)

Topping:

30g BUTTER (melted)
⅓ cup coconut
⅓ cup raw sugar
⅓ cup pecan nuts (chopped)

Method

1. Combine flour and sugar.
2. Drain peaches, reserving one third of a cup of syrup. Combine with milk, lightly beaten egg and melted butter. Add to flour and beat until smooth.
3. Pour half the batter into a lightly buttered 23cm rounc casserole dish.
4. Top with well-drained peaches. Pour remaining batter over the peaches.
5. Combine all ingredients for topping. Pour over pudding.
6. Bake (at 180°C) for 30–45 minutes (or until golden). Serve with custard.

Serves 6

Two Fruit Custard Crumble

(photographed below)

Ingredients

1 x 425g can cling peach slices
1 x 425g can pear halves (sliced)
¼ cup custard powder
1 cup BANANA FLAVOURED MILK
½ cup cornflakes
2 tablespoons coconut (shredded)
2 tablespoons brown sugar
½ teaspoon cinnamon

Method

1. Drain fruit and reserve half a cup of juice. Arrange peach and pear slices alternately in an ovenproof dish.
2. Combine custard powder and a small amount of milk together until blended.
3. Add remaining milk and reserved juice and cook (stirring continuously) until thickened.
4. Pour the custard over the fruit. Sprinkle with cornflakes, coconut, sugar and cinnamon. Grill until golden brown. Serve immediately.

Serves 4

Currant Scones

Ingredients

75g BUTTER
1 tablespoon golden syrup
3 cups self-raising flour
½ cup caster sugar
1 cup currants
1 cup MILK
¼ cup MILK (extra)

Method

1. Gently melt butter and golden syrup together.
2. Sift flour, and add sugar and currants. Mix together. Make a well in the centre. Add butter and syrup with milk. Mix to make a soft dough.
3. Turn out onto a board covered with GLAD Bake. Knead until smooth. Roll or pat out to 1½–2cm thickness. Cut with a 6cm fluted (or round) cutter. Place on an oven tray. Brush tops with extra milk.
4. Bake (at 230°C) for 10–15 minutes (or until golden on top). Serve warm with butter.

Makes 24

Two Fruit Custard Crumble

Threeberry Gelati

Choc Mint Crème

Ingredients

1½ tablespoons gelatine
3 cups MILK
3 eggs (separated)
½ cup sugar
1 teaspoon peppermint essence
100g cooking chocolate (finely chopped)
mint leaves (for garnish)

Method

1. Soak gelatine in milk for 5 minutes, then place over low heat and stir (until dissolved).
2. Beat egg yolks with sugar, then slowly stir into milk. Bring to the boil, stirring constantly. Remove from heat and stir in peppermint essence and chocolate.
3. Whip egg whites (until soft peaks form), and fold into milk mixture. Pour into wetted mould. Cool, then chill (until firm).
4. Carefully unmould onto serving dishes or chill in serving glasses. Garnish with mint leaf.

Serves 6

Three Berry Gelati

(photographed above)

Ingredients

3 cups SKIM MILK
1¼ cup caster sugar
2¼ cups SKIM MILK POWDER
1½ tablespoons lemon juice
2 teaspoons vanilla essence
250g strawberries (puréed)
250g blueberries (puréed)
250g raspberries (puréed)

Method

1. Combine milk, sugar and milk powder. Heat, stirring, until sugar has dissolved. Refrigerate until chilled.
2. Add lemon juice and vanilla essence, and divide mixture into three. Add strawberries to one portion, blueberries to the second and raspberries to the third.
3. Place in freezer trays, and freeze (until semi-frozen). Remove, break up with a fork, and refreeze. Alternatively, freeze in an ice cream churn.

Serves 8 (makes 1½ litres)

Ambrosia Whip

(photographed below)

Ingredients

1 x 140g can peaches (in natural juice)
1 tablespoon passionfruit pulp
2 teaspoons coconut (desiccated)
1 cup reduced fat MILK or REDUCED FAT EVAPORATED MILK (chilled)
1 cup apricot nectar
1 scoop VANILLA ICE CREAM
2 ice cubes (crushed)
desiccated coconut (for sprinkling)

Method

1. Blend the peaches, passionfruit and coconut together in a blender (until finely chopped).
2. Add the remaining ingredients, and blend (until thick and frothy). Serve sprinkled with extra coconut.

Serves 2

Hot Rum Punch

Ingredients

600mL MILK
1½ tablespoons cocoa (sieved)
2 teaspoons sugar
6 marshmallows (halved and toasted)
2 teaspoons rum (or to taste)

Method

1. Blend a little of the milk with combined cocoa and sugar.
2. Pour into a saucepan with the remaining milk and marshmallows. Heat gently (to simmering point). Flavour with rum.
3 Pour into mugs. Sprinkle with a little extra cocoa.

Serves 2–3

Ambrosia Whip

Cheese

Australian cheeses are versatile, tasty and nutritious, with each of the more than 60 varieties having its own special taste and texture. Cheese provides all of the nutrients of milk in a concentrated form.

Cheese is well known as a valuable source of protein, rivalling the standard high-protein foods of meat, fish and eggs. Protein is needed for its body-building properties.

Protein is an integral part of muscle and is needed to maintain muscle and tissue strength. Cheese is also a rich source of calcium. In fact, a slice of cheese, or even a small cube (3cm), provides about one-third of the recommended dietary intake of calcium.

As with wine, slight variations in the composition of cheese (and in the conditions of storage during maturation) can produce notable variations.

Australian cheeses can be enjoyed on their own or added to cooking. The large range includes many low-fat and salt-reduced varieties, and the range is growing all the time. Have a browse at your local supermarket or delicatessen.

Australians are becoming a nation of cheese eaters, influenced by our growing desire for good health and nutrition.

A cheeseboard is probably the simplest (yet most effective) way for bringing people together to discover, and enjoy, the many varieties of Australian cheeses available. Be it for a cocktail party, lunch, barbecue, dinner party or wine and cheese night, the versatility of a cheeseboard cannot be beaten.

Corn Chip Chicken Fingers with Avocado Dip

Ingredients

4 skinned chicken fillets (cut into strips)
flour (for coating)
2 eggs (lightly beaten)
1 cup natural corn chips (crushed)
1 cup REDUCED FAT CHEDDAR CHEESE (grated)
2 teaspoons chilli powder
1 avocado (peeled and stoned)
1 cup LOW FAT NATURAL YOGURT
2 teaspoons honey

Method

1. Coat the chicken strips in flour, dip in egg, and roll in mixture of corn chips, cheese and chilli powder.
2. Place on a lightly buttered oven tray and bake (at 200°C) for 10 minutes (or until golden brown).
3. Purée the avocado in a food processor (until smooth), and add the yogurt and honey.
4. Serve with the chicken fingers.

Serves 8

Mozzarella, Spinach and Sun-dried Tomato Calzone

Ingredients
2 teaspoons yeast (dried)
1 teaspoon sugar
1½ cups warm water
4½ cups plain flour
pinch salt
2 tablespoons olive oil
1 bunch fresh spinach (washed and chopped)
150g MOZZARELLA CHEESE (cubed)
125g FETA CHEESE (cubed)
¼ cup sun-dried tomatoes (chopped)
¼ cup pitted black olives

Serves 6

Method

1. Combine yeast, sugar and water together. Stand for 10 minutes (until frothy).
2. Combine flour and salt, and make a well in the centre, Mix in yeast and oil (to make a soft dough). Knead for 5 minutes (until smooth and elastic). Cover, and allow to prove in a warm place for 40 minutes (until doubled in size).
3. Cook spinach with 1 tablespoon of water in a covered pan (until softened). Cool and drain. Add cheeses, tomatoes and olives.
4. Knock back dough and divide into 8 pieces. Roll out each piece to a 15cm circle.
5. Divide the cheese mixture evenly between each circle. Moisten edges with water and fold in half to form a half moon shape.
6. Bake (at 220°C) for 20–25 minutes until golden brown.

Chilli Eggplant Moussaka

(photographed at right)

Ingredients

25g BUTTER
1 onion (chopped)
1 clove garlic (crushed)
2 teaspoons chilli (chopped)
500g lean lamb mince
1 x 440g can tomato pieces
2 tablespoons tomato paste
1 large eggplant (cut into slices)
50g BUTTER (extra)
¼ cup plain flour
3 cups MILK
¼ cup SKIM MILK POWDER
1½ cups PARMESAN CHEESE
2 large potatoes (boiled and sliced)
¼ cup bread crumbs (dried)

Method

1. Melt butter in a saucepan, and sauté onion, garlic, chilli and mince (until browned). Add tomato pieces and paste, and simmer for 5 minutes.
2. Grill eggplant slices on both sides (until golden brown).
3. Melt the extra butter in a saucepan, add the flour and cook (stirring) for 1 minute. Add the milk and milk powder, and stir (until thickened).
4. Mix in 1 cup of cheese (until melted). Layer potato slices, eggplant and mince in the base of a lasagne (or casserole) dish, and top with cheese sauce. Sprinkle with breadcrumbs and the remaining Parmesan cheese.
5. Bake (at 180°C) for 15–20 minutes until golden brown. Serve with salad.

Serves 6

Pumpkin Cheddar Chowder

(photographed at left)

Ingredients

2 rashers lean bacon (chopped)
½ leek (sliced)
500g pumpkin (peeled and chopped)
2 cups chicken stock
1 cup CHEDDAR CHEESE (grated)
1 cup MILK
2 teaspoons chives (snipped)
salt and pepper (to taste)
SOUR CREAM (for garnish)
fresh chives (for garnish)

Method

1. Sauté bacon and leek in a large saucepan for 2 minutes.
2. Add pumpkin and chicken stock, and simmer (covered) for 15 minutes (or until tender).
3. Purée in a food processor until smooth.
4. Return to a clean saucepan. Add cheese, milk and chives and season to taste. Reheat without boiling.
5. Serve with a swirl of sour cream and fresh chives for garnish.

Serves 6

Blue Vein Cheese and Chive Soufflé

(photographed below)

Ingredients

25g BUTTER
1 tablespoon plain flour
1 tablespoon mustard (seeded)
½ cup MILK
125g BLUE VEIN CHEESE (crumbled)
1 tablespoon chives (snipped)
3 eggs (separated)

Method

1. Melt butter in a saucepan. Add flour and mustard, and cook for 1 minute (stirring continuously).
2. Add milk and cook, stirring until thick and glossy. Add cheese and chives. Allow to cool slightly. Gradually beat in egg yolks.
3. Beat egg whites (until stiff peaks form), and fold into mixture.
4. Spoon into 4 buttered 1-cup soufflé dishes, and bake (at 200°C) for 15–20 minutes (or until golden brown and well risen). Serve immediately.

Serves 4

Feta Bruschetta

Ingredients

1 large red capsicum
50g BUTTER
1 clove garlic (crushed)
1 teaspoon oregano
1 French bread stick
200g FETA CHEESE (cubed)
½ cup black olives
2 spring onions (chopped)
2 tablespoons PARMESAN CHEESE (grated)

Method

1. Grill the red capsicum, turning occasionally (until blackened on all sides). Place into a paper bag to cool before peeling, deseeding and cutting into strips.
2. Melt the butter and add the garlic and oregano. Cut the French stickdiagonally into 2cm slices, and brush on both sides with garlic butter.
3. Grill on both sides until lightly toasted. Top with the capsicum, Feta, olives and spring onions, and sprinkle with Parmesan.
4. Grill for 2 minutes (until the cheese softens). Serve immediately.

Serves 6

Blue Vein Cheese and Chive Soufflé

Floral Delights

(photographed at right)

Ingredients

assorted salad leaves (equivalent to 1 lettuce)
8–10 Nasturtium flowers
¼ cup cashew nuts (toasted)
100g SWISS-STYLE CHEESE (cut into 2cm cubes)
¼ cup mustard cress
½ cup prepared French dressing

Method

1. Tear lettuce into bite-sized pieces and place in a salad bowl.
2. Toss in Nasturtiums, nuts, cheese and mustard cress.
3. Pour dressing over the dish just prior to serving.

Serves 4-6

Cheese and Noodle Toss

(photographed at left)

Ingredients

1½ cups bow noodles (cooked)
1 zucchini (sliced)
8 cherry tomatoes (halved)
½ cup chopped basil
1 cup CHEDDAR CHEESE (grated)
1 x 50g can anchovy fillets (halved)
2 tablespoons prepared French dressing

Method

1. In a salad bowl combine together the noodles, zucchini, tomato halves, basil and grated cheese.
2. Place anchovies in salad.
3. Pour in the French dressing and toss gently.

Serves 4

Colourful Garden Salad

(photographed at right)

Ingredients

salad greens (equivalent to 1 lettuce)
100g GOUDA CHEESE (cut into 1cm x 3cm sticks)
1 cucumber (sliced)
1 punnet strawberries (washed and hulled)
1 mandarin (peeled and segmented)
1 pear (cored and sliced)
100g snow peas (blanched)
rind of 1 lemon (grated)
¼ cup prepared French dressing
1 clove garlic (crushed)

Method

1. Combine together the first 7 ingredients.
2. Blend lemon rind with dressing and garlic. Shake well and pour over salad.

Serves 4-6

Fruity Coleslaw

(photographed at left)

Ingredients

½ pineapple (sliced lengthways)
1 cup cabbage (shredded)
2 sticks celery (chopped)
1 large orange (peeled and segmented)
1 bunch grapes
½ cup COTTAGE CHEESE
black pepper
¼ cup chopped mint

Method

1. Scoop out pineapple from shell (leaving shell intact), and dice pineapple flesh.
2. Combine cabbage, celery, orange, grapes and diced pineapple.
3. Season cottage cheese with pepper and mint. Toss through salad.
4. Spoon back into pineapple shell and serve.

Serves 4

Piquant Prawn Salad

(photographed at right)

Ingredients

125g BLUE VEIN CHEESE
1 tablespoon port
¼ cup SOUR CREAM
2 cups shell noodles (cooked)
100g snow peas (blanched)
2 large yellow or red capsicums (cut into matchstick-sized pieces)
50g pecan nuts (lightly toasted)
12 prawns (cooked and shelled)

Method

1. Blend cheese with port and cream to form a smooth dressing.
2. Toss noodles, snow peas, capsicum and pecan nuts in dressing.
3. Place salad on serving plates and arrange prawns on top.

Serves 2

Greek-Style Feta Feast

(photographed at left)

Ingredients

1 endive lettuce (torn into bite-sized pieces)
2 large tomatoes (quartered)
1 onion (sliced into rings)
100g hot salami (sliced into strips)
¼ continental cucumber (sliced)
½ cup black olives
150g FETA CHEESE (cubed)
1½ tablespoons basil (chopped)
¼ cup prepared Italian dressing

Method

1. Toss together lettuce, tomato, onion, salami, cucumber, olives and Feta cheese.
2. Combine basil and dressing and pour over salad.

Serves 2

Mushroom and Bacon Strudel

(photographed below)

Ingredients

20g BUTTER
4 spring onions (chopped)
4 rashers lean bacon (sliced)
450g button mushrooms (sliced)
1 x 250g tub COTTAGE CHEESE
¼ cup PARMESAN CHEESE (grated)
6 sheets filo pastry
20g BUTTER (extra, melted)
PARMESAN CHEESE (extra, for sprinkling)
paprika (for sprinkling)

Method

1. Melt butter in a saucepan and sauté spring onions and bacon (until softened). Add mushrooms and cook for 1 minute. Allow to cool and drain off excess liquid.
2. Add cottage and Parmesan cheese. Brush each sheet of pastry with butter, and layer on top of each other.
3. Place filling in centre of pastry and fold into a parcel. Place on a baking tray, brush with butter, and sprinkle with extra Parmesan and paprika.
4. Bake (at 180°C) for 25–30 minutes (or until golden brown).

Serves 6

Jan's Handy Tip

Always store mushrooms in paper bags in the refrigerator. This will stop them sweating.

Parmesan Crumbed Veal with Ratatouille Sauce

Ingredients

¾ cup PARMESAN CHEESE (grated)
¾ cup cornflake crumbs
½ teaspoon mixed herbs (dried)
4 large veal escalopes
flour (for coating)
2 eggs (lightly beaten)
30g BUTTER
1 onion (cut into cubes)
1 x 440g can peeled tomatoes (chopped)
½ cup white wine
2 tablespoons tomato paste
1 green capsicum (diced)
1 zucchini (diced)
¼ cup black olives (sliced)
steamed broccoli and corn (for serving)

Method

1. Combine the Parmesan, cornflake crumbs and mixed herbs.
2. Coat the veal in flour, dip in egg, and coat in the Parmesan mixture. Bake (at 200°C) for 15–20 minutes (until golden brown).
3. Melt the butter and sauté the onion until softened. Add the tomatoes, wine and tomato paste and bring to the boil. Allow to simmer until reduced by one third. Add the remaining ingredients and cook for a further 5 minutes.
4. Pour the sauce over the veal, and serve with steamed broccoli and corn.

Serves 6

Mushroom and Bacon Strudel

Asparagus Camembert Beef

Apricot 'n' Walnut Cutlets

Ingredients

8 lamb cutlets (trimmed)
8 rashes, bacon (rindless)

Stuffing:

¼ cup walnuts (finely chopped)
½ cup dried apricots (finely chopped
1 cup dry breadcrumbs
125g MILD CHEDDAR CHEESE (finely grated)
salt and pepper (to taste)

Method

1. Mix the Stuffing ingredients until well combined.
2. Mould a rounded teaspoon of stuffing on either side of each cutlet. Wrap each with a rasher and secure with a toothpick.
3. Place in OSO Aluminium Foil-lined shallow baking tray. Bake (at 180°C) for 45 minutes.
4. Serve with jacket potatoes, whole baked tomatoes and buttered beans.

Serves 4–6

Jan's Handy Tip

Use a piece of GLAD Bake on top of sauces or custards that have been left to cool to stop skin forming.

Asparagus Camembert Beef

(photographed above)

Ingredients

500g piece beef fillet
2 teaspoons French mustard
freshly ground black pepper (to taste)
125g CAMEMBERT or BRIE (sliced)
6 asparagus spears (blanched)
2 teaspoons Worcestershire sauce
10g BUTTER

Method

1. Make a cut down the centre of the fillet, ensuring not to cut all the way through, and open out. Spread with mustard and season with pepper.
2. Arrange the Camembert and asparagus down the centre of the fillet. Reshape and secure with skewers.
3. Sprinkle the fillet with Worcestershire sauce. Heat the butter in a heavy-based baking pan and brown the fillet on all sides.
4. Bake for 20–25 minutes for medium (or until cooked to your liking). Serve sliced hot or cold.

Serves 4

Raclette Covered Potatoes

Râclette-covered Potatoes

(photographed above)

Ingredients

2 medium Pontiac potatoes (unpeeled)
1 medium orange sweet potato (kumera) (peeled)
salt and pepper (to taste)
1½ cups RÂCLETTE* or SWISS-STYLE CHEESE (grated)
paprika (for sprinkling)

Method

1. Cut potatoes and sweet potatoes into slices. Boil or microwave until tender.
2. Arrange alternate slices onto a buttered baking tray. Season with salt and pepper to taste. Sprinkle with Râclette and paprika.
3. Bake (at 180°C) for 15 minutes (until cheese melts).

*Râclette cheese has a firm yellow body, with small 'eyes' and a brown skin. Flavour is similar to that of Swiss-style cheese—sweet and nutty. This is an excellent melting cheese which is available at delicatessens and specialty cheese shops.

Serves 4

Tuna Boat Roll

1 teaspoon BUTTER
2 long white rolls (halved horizontally)
2 tablespoons RICOTTA cheese
1 small tomato (sliced)
½ small onion (sliced)
1 stick celery (finely diced)
1 x 185g can tuna in brine (drained))
freshly ground black pepper (to taste)

Method

1. Lightly butter the top halves of the rolls. Spread the bottom halves with ricotta cheese.
2. Top the ricotta with the remaining ingredients. Close the rolls and wrap in GLAD Wrap.
3. Serve with a piece of fruit and a glass of chilled milk.

Makes 2 rolls

Jan's Handy Tip

Keep grated cheese in a GLAD SnapLock Bag in your refrigerator. A sugar cube added to the bag will keep the cheese from going mouldy.

Mustard Cheddar Chicken

(photographed below)

Ingredients

4 chicken fillets (skinned)
2 tablespoons mustard (seeded)
20g BUTTER
½ cup dry white wine
1 teaspoon rosemary
4 slices ham (e.g. Virginia or gypsy)
125g VINTAGE CHEDDAR CHEESE (grated)

Method

1. Spread chicken fillets with mustard. Melt the butter in a frying pan, and cook the chicken for 2 minutes on each side.
2. Add the wine and rosemary, cover, and cook for 5 minutes.
3. Arrange a slice of ham and grated cheese over each chicken fillet, cover, and cook for a further 5 minutes until the cheese has melted. Serve immediately.

Serves 4

Grilled Steak Fondue

Ingredients

4 slices lean rump steak

Sauce:

250g PROCESSED CHEDDAR CHEESE
1 teaspoon salt
2 cloves garlic (crushed)
½ teaspoon black pepper (freshly ground)
¾ cup tomato juice
parsley, for garnish

Method

1. Season steak to taste. Grill or barbecue (to desired liking).
2. Place sauce ingredients in a pan. Stir continually over a gentle heat until cheese melts. Simmer for several minutes. Adjust seasonings.
3. Spoon over steaks. Garnish with parsley.

Serves 4

Mustard Cheddar Chicken

Slimmer's Apricot Cheesecake

Ingredients
500g LOW FAT COTTAGE CHEESE
3 eggs
rind and juice of 1 lemon (finely grated)
½ cup apricot nectar
¾ cup LIGHT SOUR CREAM
¼ cup dried apricots (chopped)

Topping:
⅓ cup carbohydrate modified apricot jam
1 tablespoon arrowroot
2 tablespoons water

Serves 10

Method

1. Beat the cheese until smooth. Add in eggs one at a time, and beat well between each addition. Add lemon rind, lemon juice and apricot nectar.
2. Gently blend in sour cream and apricots.
3. Pour into a 18cm springform tin and bake (at 160°C) for 40 minutes. Leave cheesecake undisturbed in the oven for a further 30 minutes. Allow to cool.
4. Place jam in a saucepan and heat gently. Blend arrowroot with water to form a smooth paste. Add to jam, stir until thickened. Pour over the top of the cheesecake. Chill thoroughly.

Classical Baked Cheesecake

Ingredients
150g plain sweet biscuits (crushed)
75g BUTTER (melted)
500g COTTAGE CHEESE
or 500g CREAM CHEESE
¾ cup caster sugar
rind of 1 lemon (finely grated)
2 tablespoons lemon juice
3 eggs
300mL CREAM
fruit and cream (for decorating)

Serves 8–10

Method

1. Combine biscuits and butter together. Press firmly into base of a 20cm springform tin. Refrigerate until firm.
2. Beat cheese and sugar together (until smooth). Thoroughly beat in lemon rind, juice and eggs. Gently blend in cream. Pour into prepared tin.
3. Bake (at 160°C) for 45 minutes. Turn oven off. Leave cheesecake undisturbed in oven for a further 30 minutes. Allow to cool.
4. Chill in refrigerator for several hours. Decorate as desired with fresh or canned fruit and cream.

Blueberry Sponge Cheesecake

Ingredients
4 eggs
¾ cup caster sugar
1 cup self-raising flour (sifted)
4 tablespoons boiling water
350g NEUFCHÂTEL* cheese (softened)
100g BUTTER (softened)
⅓ cup caster sugar (extra)
½ cup almonds (ground)
2 tablespoons Galliano (or other liqueur)
1 punnet blueberries
¼ cup plum jam
icing sugar (for dusting)

Method

1. Beat eggs and sugar together until thick and creamy. Fold in flour and water.
2. Pour into a buttered and GLAD Bake- lined 24cm springform pan and bake (at 180°C) for 40–45 minutes. Remove and cool on a rack.
3. Cream Neufchâtel, butter and extra sugar together. Stir in almonds, liqueur and berries. Cut sponge in half, place one half of sponge back into springform tin. Spread with jam.
4. Top with cheese mixture. Cut remaining sponge into 12 wedges and arrange on top. Refrigerate until set. Serve dusted with icing sugar.

*Neufchâtel cheese has a smooth, spreadable texture with a creamy flavour. It is also available in chocolate and strawberry flavours. It can be obtained from delicatessens, specialty cheese shops and some supermarkets.

Serves 12

Fruit Cheese and Almond Blintzes

(photographed below)

Ingredients

1 cup plain flour
1 egg
1½ cups MILK
BUTTER (as required)
400g FRUIT CHEESE (softened)
2 tablespoons Grand Marnier
⅓ cup almonds (flaked, toasted)
1 tablespoon brown sugar
almonds (toasted, flaked; for garnish)

Method

1. Place flour in a bowl, make a well in the centre and whisk in the egg and milk to form a batter.
2. Lightly coat a crêpe pan with butter and heat. Pour a quarter of a cup of batter into the pan and swirl to coat the base.
3. Cook for 1 minute (until the underside is golden), then turn over and cook a further 30 seconds on the second side. Repeat with remaining mixture (buttering when necessary) to make 12 crêpes.
4. Blend the softened fruit cheese together with the Grand Marnier and almonds, and divide evenly between each crêpe. Fold up to form 12 parcels. Refrigerate until required.
5. Just prior to serving, sprinkle with sugar and grill until golden and warmed through. Serve garnished with toasted almonds.

Serves 6

Microwave Lemon Cheesecake

100g BUTTER
200g plain biscuits (crushed)
250g CREAM CHEESE
250g COTTAGE CHEESE
3 eggs (lightly beaten)
¾ cup sugar
1 tablespoon cornflour
½ cup SOUR CREAM
rind of 1 lemon (grated)
3 tablespoons lemon juice
3 tablespoons lemon butter

Method

1. Melt butter in a medium sized bowl on HIGH (100%) for 1 minute. Stir in biscuit crumbs and mix thoroughly. Press over the base and sides of a 21cm x 5cm round ovenproof dish. Refrigerate (while preparing filling).
2. Soften cream cheese in bowl on HIGH (100%) for 1 minute, and beat until smooth. Add cottage cheese, eggs, sugar, cornflour, sour cream, lemon rind and 1 tablespoon of the lemon juice. Beat mixture until smooth and well blended.
3. Pour onto biscuit crumbs and cook on MEDIUM/HIGH (70%) for 20 minutes. Cool before removing cheesecake from dish. Blend remaining lemon juice with lemon butter, warm on MEDIUM/LOW (30%) for 2 minutes and stir well. Pour over top of cheesecake. Chill thoroughly before serving.

Serves 8

Fruit Cheese and Almond Blintzes

Strawberry Tiramisù

Ingredients

375g MASCARPONE*CHEESE
½ cup PURE CREAM
2 egg yolks
2 tablespoons caster sugar
1 cup hot strong black coffee (or espresso)
2 tablespoons caster sugar (extra)
¾ cup marsala
500g sponge finger biscuits
1 cup strawberries (sliced)
cocoa (for dusting)

Method

1. Beat the Mascarpone, cream, yolks and sugar together (until stiff).
2. Combine the coffee, extra sugar and marsala together, and cool.
3. Dip half of the biscuits in the coffee syrup, and layer in a serving dish. Spread half of the Mascarpone mixture on this, and top with strawberries.
4. Layer remaining dipper biscuits and Mascarpone on top.
5. Dust with cocoa and refrigerate for at least an hour before serving.

*Mascarpone cheese has a smooth, whipped cream texture and a slightly 'tart' creamy flavour. It is available at delicatessens, specialty cheese shops and some supermarkets.

Serving Suggestion: Pipe Mascarpone mixture onto biscuits which have been dipped in coffee mixture. Layer with strawberries, and sandwich 2 biscuits on top of each other. Dust with cocoa.

Serves 12

Yogurt

Yogurt has been enjoyed around the world for centuries. It was perhaps the first 'health food'. 'Yogurt' is a Turkish word for fermented milk which is known in many countries under different names. In Egypt, for example, it is called 'Leben', a name that has also appeared in Australia. Like milk, yogurt is rich in nutrients, but it has a unique, tangy taste resulting from the way it is made.

A Unique Blend

Yogurt is a unique blend of nutritious milk and beneficial bacterial cultures. It appeals to all ages and tastes.

The beneficial bacterial cultures which are used in production of yoghurt enhance flavour and aroma, while other bacterial cultures, such as *lactobacillus acidophilus* and *bifidobacterium* (known simply as A and B cultures) are added for their benefits to health.

Skim milks can be used to produce a virtually no-fat, smooth and tasty yogurt, while regular milk produces rich, creamy yogurts, high in taste appeal. Although high in taste appeal, regular yogurt is lower in fat than most people think, with a fat content of less than 4 per cent.

Reduced fat yogurt contains only 1–2 per cent fat, and low-fat and skim milk yogurt contains not more than .per cent fat.

For Calcium Needs

Yogurt is high in nutrition because it is made from milk. Extra skim milk is added during the production of yogurt which results in increased protein and calcium content, while generally lowering the fat content.

Like milk and cheese, yogurt is a rich source of calcium. Calcium is a very important mineral, much needed by the body, with around 99 per cent being found in the skeleton and teeth, and the remaining 1 per cent in the blood and body fluids.

Calcium is needed for the development and growth of strong bones and teeth. An adequate daily intake of calcium is obviously required by children, but it is also required by adults (especially women) to help prevent osteoporosis.

A long-term balanced diet incorporating three serves of dairy food per day—a serve is equal to a 250mL glass of milk, a 200g tub of Yogurt, a 40g piece of hard yellow cheese, or any combination of these three foods—provides most people with the recommended dietary intake of calcium needed per day. This dietary intake, together with moderate weight-bearing exercise, helps to prevent osteoporosis.

Can Help Some Health Problems

The rich nutrient content, and the effects of its friendly bacterial cultures, are yogurt's prime health benefits. Medical researchers believe yogurt may have a beneficial role in many health problems:

- Yogurt is believed to help normalise gut function following a course of antibiotics.
- The lactic acid bacteria in yogurt have a settling effect on the stomach by decreasing harmful bacteria in the intestine.
- Research has shown that yogurt with B culture added may have a beneficial effect upon constipation and diarrhoea.
- Recent US research has shown that eating 250g of lactobacillus acidophilus (A culture) yogurt daily decreases candidal vaginitis ('thrush' infection).
- Yogurt can be a useful source of calcium for people diagnosed as being lactose intolerant. Those with lactose intolerance are deficient in the lactose-digesting intestinal enzyme, lactase, but may be able to digest the lactose in yogurt more efficiently than the same amount of lactose in milk. Yogurt has a lower lactose content than milk, and is digested more slowly.

Types of Yogurt

- 'Natural' Yogurt has no added flavours or sweetening, and is enjoyed by those who appreciate its fresh tang. It has many uses in cooking.
- Flavoured Yogurt is natural yogurt to which has been added flavourings such as vanilla, strawberry or chocolate, and sugar or artificial sweetener.
- Fruit Yogurt has fresh fruit pieces, sugar or sweetened fruit pulp added. Berries, fruit salad and apricot are popular.
- Soft serve and frozen yogurts are yogurts made from natural stirred yogurt with added fruit or flavour. They are blended to resemble reduced fat ice cream, but retain the natural yogurt flavour and tang.
- Yogurts with beneficial A and B cultures added during production are widely available throughout Australia.
- Yogurts are available with varying levels of fat—regular, reduced and low-fat (skim).

Basil, Avocado and Tomato Dip

Ingredients
¼ cup basil leaves (fresh)
2 spring onions (chopped)
1 avocado (peeled and stoned)
1 x 200g tub NATURAL YOGURT
1 small tomato (seeded and diced)
natural corn chips (for serving)

Serves 8 (makes 1½ cups)

Method

1. Place the basil and spring onions in a food prcessor, and blend (until finely chopped).
2. Add the avocado and yogurt, and blend (until smooth). Fold in the tomato.
3. Refrigerate until required. Serve with natural corn chips.

Tuna Tomato Appetisers

Tuna Tomato Appetisers

(photographed above)

Ingredients

8 medium ripe tomatoes
1 x 180g can tuna (drained)
2 spring onions (chopped)
½ red capsicum (finely diced)
½ cup white rice (cooked)
½ cup NATURAL YOGURT
1 tablespoon light French dressing
1 tablespoon basil (fresh, chopped)
freshly ground black pepper (to taste)

Method

1. Cut the tops off the tomatoes, and reserve. Hollow out the centres.
2. Combine together the tuna, spring onions, red capsicum and rice.
3. Whisk together yogurt, dressing and basil, and season to taste. Stir through tuna mixture.
4. Fill tomatoes with tuna mixture and replace tops. Serve chilled.

Serves 4

Vegetarian Hors d'œuvres

Ingredients

180g CREAM CHEESE
½ cup NATURAL YOGURT
1 tablespoon pesto sauce
1 tablespoon mayonnaise
1 tablespoon tomato paste
½ punnet cherry tomatoes (halved)
1 baby cucumber (cut into 2cm-slices)
1 stalk celery (cut into 2.5cm-lengths)
chopped red capsicum (for garnish)
chopped fresh basil (for garnish)
sliced olives (for garnish)

Method

1. Whisk cream cheese and yogurt together until smooth. Divide into three portions.
2. Add pesto to one portion, mayonnaise to the second portion, and tomato paste to the third.
3. Arrange the cherry tomato halves, cucumber slices and celery pieces on a serving plate, and place a different variety of cream cheese mixture on each. Garnish with capsicum, basil and olives.

Makes 20

Spicy Seafood Skewers with Piquant Yogurt Sauce

(photographed below)

Ingredients

12 green prawns (shelled and deveined)
12 scallops (debearded)
1 large red capsicum (cut into cubes)
2 teaspoons curry powder
2 spring onions (chopped)
1 clove garlic (crushed)
1 x 200g tub NATURAL YOGURT
¼ cup tomato sauce
1 teaspoon Worcestershire sauce
2 teaspoons cornflour

Method

1. Thread prawns, scallops and red capsicum onto skewers and sprinkle with curry.
2. Cook in a non-stick pan for 2 minutes on each side (until cooked), and remove.
3. Add the spring onions and garlic to the pan and cook (until softened).
4. Combine the remaining ingredients together and add to the pan, simmer until heated, and serve over skewers.

Alternative: Substitute 2 chicken fillets (cut into cubes) for the seafood.

Serves 4

Muffuletta Rolls

Ingredients

8 round rolls
16 lettuce leaves

Swiss Avocado Filling:

4 thin slices cold roast beef, ham or salami
1 tablespoon mayonnaise
4 thin slices SWISS-STYLE CHEESE
1 tomato (sliced)
1 avocado (diced)
lemon juice (to taste)

Curried Chicken Filling:

1 cup cooked chicken (chopped)
¼ cup APRICOT YOGURT
1 teaspoon curry powder
1 cup coleslaw
1 stalk celery (sliced)

Method

1. Cut the tops off the rolls, and hollow-out the centre. Place a lettuce leaf in each roll.
2. Mix the ingredients for each filling until well combined.
3. For each roll place a good quantity of filling on the lettuce leaf, then place another lettuce leaf on top, and replace top half of roll. Wrap tightly in foil. Refrigerate until required.

Serve cut in half, allowing one of each variety per person.

Makes 8

Spicy Seafood Skewers with Piquant Yogurt Sauce

Potato and Spinach Salad with Mustard Yogurt Dressing

(photographed below)

Ingredients

500g new potatoes (unpeeled)
50g fresh young spinach leaves (washed)
½ red capsicum (sliced)
1 salad onion (sliced)
½ cup LOW FAT NATURAL YOGURT
¼ cup SKIM MILK
¼ cup light mayonnaise
2 teaspoons wholegrain mustard
2 tablespoons parsley (chopped)
salt and pepper (to taste)

Method

1. Cook the potatoes in a saucepan of boiling water for 15 minutes (or until just tender) and then cut in half. Add the spinach, red capsicum and onion.
2. Combine the yogurt, milk, mayonnaise, mustard and parsley to form a dressing, and season to taste.
3. Pour the dressing over the potatoes, and refrigerate (until chilled). Serve.

Serves 4

Saucy Chicken Balls

Ingredients

400g chicken (skinless, minced)
200g tub HERB FLAVOURED, LOW FAT COTTAGE CHEESE
1 medium onion (chopped)
¼ cup breadcrumbs (dry)
3 teaspoons Worcestershire sauce
1 x 440g can condensed mushroom soup
200g tub LOW FAT YOGURT
1 tablespoon cornflour
250g packet pasta of choice

Method

1. Mix first 5 ingredients together in a food processor until well blended.
2. Shape into 40 small (or 15 larger) balls. Cook in a non-stick frypan until browned all over and cooked through (approximately 10–15 minutes).
3. Cook pasta according to instructions on packet. Drain.
4. Remove chicken from pan. Add soup, and stir to dissolve caramelised meat juices. Blend yogurt with cornflour (until smooth), add to soup, and stir (until thickened), but do not boil.
5. Return chicken to pan and heat through. Serve over pasta.

Serves 5

Potato and Spinach Salad with Mustard Yogurt Dressing

Apricot Chicken Sauté

(photographed below)

Ingredients

25g BUTTER
1 onion (sliced)
4 chicken fillets (cut into strips)
1 red capsicum (chopped)
2 stalks celery (sliced)
½ cup apricots (chopped and dried, soaked in ¼ cup orange juice)
1 x 200g tub APRICOT FLAVOURED YOGURT
1 tablespoon cornflour
1 tablespoon cashew nuts (roasted)

Method

1. Melt butter in wok, and sauté onion and chicken (until cooked). Add red capsicum and celery, and stir-fry (until softened).
2. Stir in apricots and juice. Combine yogurt and cornflour together, and stir into chicken with cashews.
3. Heat gently (without boiling).

Serves 4

Curried Yogurt Chicken Salad

Ingredients

1 cup LOW FAT YOGURT
½ teaspoon curry powder
rind of 1 orange (grated)
1 tablespoon orange juice (fresh)
2 spring onions (chopped)
½ red capsicum (chopped)
1 stalk celery (chopped)
1 orange (cut into segments)
2 cooked chicken fillets (cut into strips)
lettuce leaves (for serving)

Method

1. Combine the yogurt, curry powder, orange rind and juice together to form a dressing.
2. Combine all the remaining ingredients together (except for lettuce), and drizzle over the dressing.
3. Serve in lettuce cups.

Serves 4

Apricot Chicken Sauté

Apple Strudel Muffins

Apple Strudel Muffins

(photographed above)

Ingredients

1½ cups self-raising flour
⅓ cup raw sugar
1 teaspoon cinnamon
1 egg
2 x 200g tubs FRUIT SALAD YOGURT
400g can pie apple (chopped)
¼ cup sultanas
¼ cup walnuts or pecan nuts (chopped)
½ teaspoon cinnamon (extra)
2 teaspoons raw sugar (extra)

Method

1. Combine flour, sugar and cinnamon together.
2. Make a well in the centre, and mix in egg, yogurt, apple and sultanas. Spoon into 12 buttered muffin tins.
3. Combine remaining ingredients and sprinkle over muffins.
4. Bake (at 180°C) for 35–40 minutes. Serve warm or cold.

Makes 12

Apple Sultana Loaf

Ingredients

3 cups self-raising flour (sifted)
3 teaspoons mixed spice
½ cup brown sugar
2 eggs (beaten)
200g LOW FAT FRUIT YOGURT
1 apple (unpeeled, grated)
½ cup sultanas
2 tablespoons almonds (slivered, toasted)
CREAM CHEESE (for serving)

Method

1. Combine flour, mixed spice and sugar in a large mixing bowl. Make a well in the centre, stir in combined eggs and yogurt.
2. Add apple, sultanas and almonds, mixing thoroughly.
3. Place mixture into a 20cm ringpan. Bake (at 200°C) for 25 minutes (or until cooked). Allow to cool slightly before turning out. Glaze with warmed honey if desired, and serve sliced with cream cheese.

Serves 8

Banana Nut Pancakes with Sweet Yogurt Sauce

(photographed below)

Ingredients

½ cup self-raising flour
1 teaspoon cinnamon
1 egg
1½ cups NATURAL YOGURT
1 banana (mashed)
2 tablespoons walnuts (chopped)
30g BUTTER (melted)
2 tablespoons honey
walnuts (chopped, for garnish)
banana (sliced, for garnish)

Method

1. Combine flour and cinnamon. Add egg, and gradually mix in 1 cup yogurt (to form a thick batter). Stir in banana and walnuts.
2. Lightly brush a non-stick pan with butter and heat. Pour ¼ cup mixture into the pan to form a thick pancake, and cook (over low heat) for 3 minutes (or until golden). Repeat with remaining mixture.
3. Whisk remaining yogurt and honey together, and serve over pancakes. Garnish with walnuts and banana.

Serves 4

Banana Coconut Frozen Yogurt

Ingredients

500g LOW FAT VANILLA YOGURT
3 bananas (mashed)
¼ cup sugar
¼ cup coconut (desiccated)
375mL EVAPORATED REDUCED FAT MILK (well chilled)
fresh fruit (for serving)

Method

1. Mix yogurt, bananas, sugar and coconut together.
2. Whip evaporated milk (until thick and creamy). Fold in yogurt mixture, pour into ice cream trays and freeze (for at least 2 hours).
3. Whip again until frothy. Freeze until solid. Serve with fresh fruit.

Serves 8

Jan's Handy Tip

Yogurt makes a healthy, nutritious snack alternative for both children and adults. It is a useful way of adding nutrition and interest to the diets of children and elderly people, especially those with 'sensitive' stomachs.

Many yogurts have artificial sweetener added to further reduce kilojoules.

Banana Nut Pancakes with Sweet Yogurt Sauce

Tropical Yogurt Flan (Microwave)

Ingredients

Crust:

100g BUTTER
250g packet chocolate ripple biscuits (crushed)
1 egg yolk

Filling:

2 tablespoons custard powder
2 tablespoons caster sugar
1 cup MILK
3 teaspoons gelatine
2 tablespoons hot water
½ cup pineapple juice
200g TROPICAL YOGURT
shredded coconut

Serves 8

Method

1. Melt butter (on HIGH) for 50 seconds. Add biscuit crumbs and egg yolk, and press into base and sides of a buttered 25cm pie-dish. Cook (on MEDIUM/HIGH) for 1 minute.
2. Combine custard powder, sugar and milk and cook (on MEDIUM/HIGH) for 4 minutes, stirring twice during cooking.
3. Dissolve gelatine in water, and combine custard, gelatine and pineapple juice. Cool slightly, then add yogurt.
4. Whisk until smooth. Pour into piecrust, and chill (until set). Top with shredded coconut.

Marshmallow Fruit Salad Brulée

(photographed at right)

Ingredients

1 cup NATURAL YOGURT
1 orange (segmented)
1 red apple (cored and cubed)
1 banana (sliced)
1 x 440g can pineapple pieces (unsweetened, drained)
1 x 100g packet raspberry marshmallows
1 tablespoon light brown sugar

Method

1. Combine yogurt, orange segments, apple, banana, pineapple pieces and marshmallows in an ovenproof pie dish. Sprinkle with brown sugar, and grill (until golden brown).

Serves 6

Marshmallow Fruit Salad Brulée

Chocolate Cheesecake Cups

Chocolate Cheesecake Cups

(photographed at right)

Ingredients

6 chocolate ripple biscuits (finely crushed)
250g CREAM CHEESE
1 cup VANILLA YOGURT
100g dark chocolate bits
½ cup mixed dried fruit

Method

1. Divide the crushed biscuits evenly between 4 flat-based glasses. Blend the cheese and yogurt in a food processor (until smooth).

2. Heat the chocolate over simmering water (until melted). Stir a little of the cream cheese mixture into the chocolate before folding the chocolate and half of the dried fruit back into the cheese mixture.

3. Pour into glasses and decorate with remaining dried fruit. Refrigerate until set.

Serves 4

White Hot Chocolate

(photographed at right)

Ingredients

2 cups reduced fat MILK
100g white chocolate (chopped)
chocolate powder (for sprinkling)

Method

1. Heat the milk and chocolate in a saucepan (until the chocolate has melted and the milk is hot). Alternatively, heat in a microwave (on HIGH) for 3 minutes, stirring occasionally.

2. Using an electric beater, whisk (until frothy).

3. Using a spoon to hold back the froth, pour the milk into 2 mugs, and spoon the remaining froth on top. Sprinkle with chocolate powder (and serve immediately).

Serves 2

White Hot Chocolate

Strawberry Almond Smoothie

Ingredients
1 tablespoon almonds (flaked or slivered)
1 cup fresh strawberries (hulled)
1 x 200g tub STRAWBERRY YOGURT
½ cup SKIM MILK
1 scoop VANILLA ICE CREAM
extra strawberries (for garnish)

Serves 2

Method

1. Place almonds in a non-stick pan, and dry fry (until toasted). Blend in a food processor or blender (until finely chopped).
2. Add the strawberries, and blend (until smooth). Add the remaining ingredients, and blend (until thick and frothy).
3. Serve garnished with strawberries.

Fruit Salad Mousse

Ingredients
2 x 850g cans fruit salad
1 tablespoon gelatine
2 x 200g tubs LOW FAT FRUIT YOGURT (e.g. fruit salad, apricot)
600mL carton VANILLA CUSTARD

Method
1. Drain fruit from 1 can, and reserve ½ cup syrup. Purée fruit in a blender or food processor.
2. Sprinkle gelatine over syrup, and dissolve over low heat, or microwave on HIGH (100%) for 1 minute.
3. Add gelatine mixture, yogurt and custard to fruit and blend (until smooth).
4. Alternate mousse and extra fruit salad into serving glasses, and refrigerate (until set).

Serves 6

Ice Cream

Centuries before the invention of the freezer, the Chinese and Arabs were enjoying a delicacy made with whipped and frozen cream or milk. The Romans also enjoyed snow mixed with fruit, cream and honey.

Factory production of ice cream began in 1851, and today it is one of the most popular manufactured dairy products.

Ice Cream's Food Value

Ice cream is easily digested and very satisfying and, if consumed in moderation, can be part of a balanced diet. Because ice cream contains fat and sugar, moderation is important. However, in a diet featuring plenty of fresh fruits, vegetables, bread, lean meats, fish, chicken, eggs, nuts and cereals, two scoops of regular ice cream amount to no more than 5 per cent of the total dietary intake of energy.

Ice cream is very filling, so you can be easily satisfied with a reasonably sized serve. Two small scoops of regular ice cream (100mL or 50g) per day provide 56mg of calcium, 9.4g of total carbohydrate, 4.9g of fat, 0.1mg of riboflavin and only 379 kilojoules.

The food value of ice cream is similar to that of milk and, as such, its major contributions to a balanced diet are carbohydrates and calcium, together with a moderate amount of the fat needed to provide energy.

An adequate daily calcium intake is needed to build and maintain strong, healthy bones and teeth—especially important for children. It also helps to keep nerves, muscles and the normal blood-clotting function working at peak efficiency. The proteins in milk build body and muscle tissue, and the body does require a moderate amount of fat for energy (again especially important for children).

Given the calcium, carbohydrate and food values of ice cream, it makes a good, quick snack or dessert alternative for growing children, as well as for adults.

When making ice cream, an electric ice cream machine, which whips and freezes the ingredients, is ideal for achieving the correct texture.

Care and Storage

- It is recommended that ice cream not be melted or softened and then refrozen, as it will lose its rich, creamy texture.
- At the shop, buy ice cream last and transport it home using an insulated carrybag.
- Once you have served some of the ice cream, quickly return the rest to the freezer.

Making your own Basic Dairy Ice cream

Ingredients

600mL MILK
1 vanilla pod
6 egg yolks
175g sugar
600mL FRESH WHIPPING CREAM

Method

1. Bring the milk and vanilla pod almost to the boil. Take off the heat, and leave for a minimum of 15 minutes.
2. Beat egg yolks and sugar together, stir in milk and strain back into pan. Cook this custard gently over a low heat, stirring until it coats the back of a wooden spoon. Do not boil.
3. Pour into a chilled, shallow freezer container, and leave to cool. Place in freezer for about 2 hours (or until mushy).
4. Turn out into a large, chilled basin and mash with a flat whisk or fork. Lightly whip the fresh cream, and fold into the mixture. Freeze again (until mushy) and repeat the mashing process.
5. Return to freezer (to allow to firm).

Note: Do not whip the fresh cream if using an electrical or mechanical ice cream maker. Agitate chilled custard and unwhipped cream together.

Variations:

For chocolate ice cream, break up a 175g bar of plain chocolate, heat with the milk, whisking until smooth.

For strawberry ice cream, purée 350g of strawberries with 25g icing sugar and 2 teaspoons of lemon juice, and stir into made custard.

Serves 6–8

Ice Cream Cookie Sandwiches

Ingredients
2 cups self-raising flour
½ cup cocoa
¼ cup caster sugar
125g BUTTER (cubed)
1 egg (lightly beaten)
⅔ cup SOUR CREAM
1 litre ICE CREAM (chocolate ripple, chocolate, or vanilla)
icing sugar and chocolate curls (for garnish)

Method

1. Combine the flour, cocoa and sugar in a food processor, and blend (until combined). Add butter and blend (until evenly distributed).
2. Add egg and sour cream, and blend lightly (until the mixture forms a ball).
3. Roll out to 1cm thickness, between sheets of GLAD Bake.
4. Cut into rounds using an 8–10cm cutter, and place on an oven tray. Bake (at 220°C) for 15–20 minutes. Allow to cool.
5. To serve, sandwich chocolate cookies together with scoops of ice cream, and dust with icing sugar. Garnish with chocolate curls.

Serves 6

Cassata

Ingredients

½ cup glacé fruit (chopped, mixed)
2 tablespoons brandy
300mL FRESH CREAM
2 tablespoons caster sugar
125g dark chocolate
15g BUTTER
2 litre carton VANILLA ICE CREAM
1 teaspoon vanilla
2 teaspoons cocoa
125g flaked almonds (toasted)
300mL carton FRESH CREAM (extra)
wafer biscuits (for decoration)

Method

1. Combine glacé fruits and brandy, and mix well. Let stand for approximately 10 minutes. Whip cream and sugar (until thick), and fold in fruit and brandy. Spread cream mixture over base of springform pan. Freeze.
2. Put chopped chocolate and butter in top of double saucepan, stir over gently simmering water (until melted), and allow to cool.
3. Combine half of the softened ice cream and vanilla. Add approximately half a cup of this ice cream to melted chocolate mixture, and mix well. (The melted chocolate gives the ice cream a 'chocolate chip' texture). Stir in sifted cocoa, and mix well. Spread chocolate ice cream over cream, and freeze.
4. Spread remaining softened ice cream over chocolate layer, and freeze (until firm). Decorate with extra whipped cream, almonds and wafer biscuits.

Serves 6–8

Ice Cream Mud Pie with Chocolate Grasshopper Sauce

(photographed right)

Ingredients

⅓ cup REDUCED CREAM
50g dark chocolate (chopped)
1 teaspoon Creme de Menthe liqueur
1 teaspoon Creme de Cacao liqueur
4 shortcrust pastry tart shells
1 litre ICE CREAM (chocolate, coffee or vanilla)
12 marshamallows
¼ cup pecan nuts
4 ice cream wafers

Method

1. Bring the cream to the boil in a saucepan. Whisk in the chocolate (until melted), and cool. Stir in liqueurs.
2. Arrange a scoop of each ice cream, 3 marshmallows and pecan nuts in each pastry shell.
3. Drizzle with chocolate sauce and garnish with a wafer. Serve immediately.

Serves 4

Jan's Handy Tip

Remember, too much alcohol in the ice cream will stop it freezing well.

Chocolate Ice Cream Balls

Ingredients

2 litre carton VANILLA ICE CREAM
250g dark cooking chocolate
60g copha
⅓ cup Tia Maria or Kahlúa liqueur
300mL carton FRESH CREAM

Method

1. Place a flat tray in freezer for about 10 minutes. Scoop neat dome shapes of ice cream onto chilled flat tray. If ice cream softens too quickly, return tray to freezer and use another chilled tray. Freeze ice cream until solid (several hours or overnight).
2. Combine chopped chocolate copha and liqueur in top half of double saucepan. Melt over hot water, and cool to lukewarm.
3. Using 2 spoons, dip ice cream domes in chocolate as quickly as possible. Place back on a chilled tray, and return to freezer.
4. When all domes are chocolate coated, join 2 together using a little of the remaining chocolate mixture. Serve as a sauce over the ice cream balls with whipped cream.

Serves 4

Kiwifruit Super Cup

Ingredients
6 kiwifruit
1 tablespoon orange marmalade
1 tablespoon orange liqueur
½ teaspoon vanilla sugar
6 large VANILLA ICE CREAM balls
6 large STRAWBERRY ICE CREAM balls

Method

1. Peel the kiwifruit, and cut 2 of them lengthwise (into halves) and horizontally into slices. Cut the remaining 4 kiwifruit into pieces and mash them with a fork (do not purée). Mix well with the orange marmalade, orange liqueur and vanilla sugar.
2. Fill the differently coloured ice cream balls into well-chilled glasses. Decorate the spaces in between the balls with the halved kiwifruit slices so that the lighter centre parts show.
3. Pour the prepared kiwifruit sauce with a tablespoon over the ice cream, and serve immediately.

Serves 4

Strawberry Sundae Royale

Strawberry Sundae Royale

Ingredients *(photographed above)*

1½ cups strawberries (hulled)
¼ cup caster sugar
8 small sponge finger biscuits
2 tablespoons port
4 scoops STRAWBERRY ICE CREAM
4 scoops VANILLA ICE CREAM
1 banana (sliced)
2 teaspoons shredded coconut

Method

1. Chop 1 cup strawberries, and halve the remainder.
2. Combine chopped strawberries and sugar in a saucepan, and simmer (until sugar has dissolved). Boil for 5–10 minutes until thick and syrupy. Cool.
3. Dip biscuits in port. Arrange 1 scoop of strawberry ice cream, 1 scoop of vanilla, 2 biscuits, a few slices of banana and reserved strawberries in 4 serving dishes.
4. Pour over the strawberry sauce, and garnish with coconut.

Serves 4

Jan's Handy Tip

Always return ice cream to the freezer quickly after use. If allowed to melt, large ice crystals can form, destroying the smooth creamy texture.

Rocky Road Ice Cream

Ingredients

¼ cup water (boiling)
⅓ cup cocoa (sifted)
½ cup caster sugar
375mL carton FRESH CREAM (chilled)
1 teaspoon vanilla essence
½ cup THICKENED CREAM
50g dark chocolate (grated)
1 x 100g packet marshmallows (chopped)
½ cup pecan nuts (chopped)
¼ cup red glacé cherries (chopped)

Method

1. Combine water, cocoa and sugar together. Allow to cool.
2. Whip cream with vanilla (until thick), then beat in thickened cream and cocoa mixture.
3. Fold in remaining ingredients.
4. Pour into ice cream machine, and churn until blades stop turning (or for approximately 30 minutes). Spoon into container, and freeze (until ready to serve).

Makes about 1 litre

Strawberries and Cream Ice Cream

Ingredients

3 egg yolks
¼ cup caster sugar
375mL carton FRESH CREAM
1 teaspoon vanilla essence
1 cup THICKENED CREAM (whipped)
1 punnet strawberries (hulled and quartered)
4 tablespoons strawberry topping

Method

1. Beat egg yolks and sugar (until thick).
2. Heat fresh cream gently. When mildly warm, combine with egg mixture in the top of a double saucepan.
3. Whisk over simmering water (until slightly thickened). Allow to cool.
4. Fold in remaining ingredients, and pour into ice cream machine. Churn until blades stop turning.
5. Serve immediately (or freeze in an ice cube tray). Cut into triangles, and serve with strawberries.

Makes about 1 litre

Tartufi Ice Cream Truffles

(photographed below)

Ingredients

500mL CHOCOLATE or VANILLA ICE CREAM
100g dark chocolate (grated)
2 tablespoons toasted coconut (desiccated)
¼ cup toasted almonds (slivered, finely chopped)
2 tablespoons glacé cherries (finely chopped)
extra glacé cherries (halved, for garnish)

Method

1. Using a small ice cream scoop, scoop the ice cream into balls. Place on a foil-lined tray, and immediately return to the freezer (until firm).
2. Combine remaining ingredients together and quickly roll each ice cream ball in the mixture. Return to freezer (until just prior to serving).
3. Serve skewered with fancy toothpicks and extra cherry halves.

Makes 24

Jan's Handy Tip

As around 70 per cent of its food solids come from milk, ice cream provides a useful contribution to the diet as it includes the valuable milk proteins and minerals, (particularly calcium and vitamins). The usual serving of 2 scoops of natural ice cream provides only 400 kilojoules. This is much lower than many other snack foods, and only a small proportion (about 5 per cent), of the daily energy intake from a nutritionally sound, well-balanced diet.

Tartufi Ice Cream Truffles

Tropical Ice Cream Bombe

Ingredients
1 Swiss roll
6 canned pineapple rings
1 litre ICE CREAM (vanilla, passionfruit or lemon)
4 egg whites
⅔ cup caster sugar
1 tablespoon almonds (flaked)

Method
1. Cut the Swiss roll into 6 slices, and place on a GLAD Bake-lined tray. Top each slice with a pineapple ring.
2. Place a large scoop of ice cream in the centre of each pineapple ring, and immediately return tray to freezer. Freeze until required.
3. Preheat oven (to 200°C). Just before serving, beat egg whites (until stiff peaks form), and gradually beat in sugar.
4. Working quickly, cover each ball of ice cream completely with meringue, sprinkle with almonds, and bake for 2–3 minutes (until the meringue is lightly golden). Serve immediately.

Serves 2

Sunshine Sundae with Dried Apricot Sauce

Sunshine Sundae with Dried Apricot Sauce

(photographed above)

Ingredients

½ cup apricots (dried)
¼ cup fresh orange juice
1 tablespoon honey
4 ripe bananas (peeled)
1 litre VANILLA ICE CREAM
1 x 440g can unsweetened pineapple thins (drained)
2 tablespoons shredded coconut (toasted)
almond bread or ice cream wafers (for serving)

Method

1. Simmer apricots n the orange juice and honey (until soft). Purée in a blender or food processor (until smooth).
2. Split the bananas in half (lengthwise).
3. Assemble sundaes in 4 serving dishes using banana halves, 2–3 scoops vanilla ice cream and pineapple thins.
4. Drizzle with dried apricot sauce, and sprinkle with coconut. Serve with almond bread.
5. **Sauce Microwave Method:** Cook the apricots, orange juice and honey on HIGH (100%) for 2–3 minutes (or until soft). Proceed as above.

Serves 4

Boysenberry Swirl Ice Cream

Ingredients

4 egg yolks
½ cup caster sugar
375mL carton FRESH CREAM
1 teaspoon vanilla essence
425g can boysenberries (drained)
1 cup THICKENED CREAM
1 teaspoon gelatine (dissolved in 1 tablespoon boiling water)

Method

1. Beat egg yolks and sugar together.
2. Gently heat cream, and combine with egg yolk mixture in the top of a double saucepan. Whisk over the simmering water (until slightly thickened). Allow to cool.
3. Add vanilla, half of the boysenberries, and the thickened cream. Pour into ice cream machine and churn (until firm).
4. Purée the remaining boysenberries in processor (or blender), with the dissolved gelatine. Spoon ice cream into a container, and lightly fold in the puréed boysenberries (to give a swirled appearance). Serve immediately.

Makes about 1 litre

Low Fat Kiwifruit and Orange Ice Cream Slice

Low Fat Kiwifruit and Orange Ice cream Slice

(photographed above)

Ingredients

6 LOW CALORIE ICE CREAM SLICES
12 ice cream wafer biscuits
1 orange (peeled and sliced thinly)
1 kiwifruit (peeled and sliced)
¼ cup passionfruit pulp

Method

1. Place an ice cream slice on each of 6 wafer biscuits.
2. Arrange alternate slices of orange and kiwifruit on top, and drizzle with passionfruit.
3. Top with remaining wafers. Serve immediately.

Serves 4

Gianduia

Ingredients

750mL VANILLA ICE CREAM
⅓ cup cocoa powder
½ cup toasted hazelnuts (chopped)
extra sugar (to taste)

Method

1. Ensure ice cream is soft, then fold in cocoa, hazelnuts and sugar. Mix well.
2. Pour into a wetted mould, and allow to set. This ice cream should be served semi-frozen (so it has a mousse-like consistency).

Serves 6–8

Creamy Honey Ice Cream

Ingredients
3 egg yolks
1 egg
375mL FRESH CREAM
200mL honey
300mL THICKENED CREAM (whipped)

Method

1. Combine egg yolks and egg in the top of a double saucepan, and beat (until light and fluffy).
2. Heat cream in a saucepan (until lukewarm). Stir in honey, and gradually whisk in egg mixture. Stir constantly over simmering water (until slightly thickened).
3. Remove from heat, and allow to cool. Fold through whipped cream, pour into ice cream machine, and churn (until firm).

Serve immediately (or turn into a GLAD TuckAway Foil Tray and freeze).

Makes about 1 litre

Pink Strawberry Spider

Ingredients

200mL chilled red lemonade (or 200mL chilled lemonade) and 1 tablespoon strawberry topping
2 scoops STRAWBERRY ICE CREAM

Serves 1

Method

1. Pour the lemonade into a long glass.
2. Place 1 scoop of ice cream in the lemonade, and stir lightly. Position the other scoop on the rim.
3. Garnish with straws and a parfait spoon, and serve immediately.

Banana Colada Shake

Ingredients
1 banana (chopped)
½ cup MILK (chilled)
¼ teaspoon rum essence (or 2 tablespoons white rum)
2 tablespoons coconut (dessicated)
½ cup pineapple juice
2 scoops VANILLA ICE CREAM
2–3 tablespoons crushed ice
toasted coconut and extra ice cream (for garnishing)

Method
1. Place all the ingredients in a blender, and blend (until well combined).
2. Pour into 2 tulip-shaped colada glasses.
3. Garnish with toasted coconut and extra ice cream.

Serves 2

Grand Marnier Cream

Ingredients

½ cup sugar
¼ cup orange juice
½ cup water
1 teaspoon grated orange peel
8 egg yolks
¼ cup Grand Marnier liqueur
1 cup WHIPPING CREAM

Method

1. In a heavy-based saucepan, combine sugar, orange juice, water and peel. Stir constantly over a medium heat (until mixture comes to a boil). Cook rapidly for 5 minutes. Set aside.
2. Beat egg yolks until fluffy and pale lemon coloured. Beating constantly, pour hot syrup over beaten egg yolks. Continue beating, and cook over hot water (until mixture is very thick), then cool.
3. Fold in Grand Marnier liqueur.
4. Whip cream (until soft peaks form) and fold into egg mixture. Pour into ice cream maker, and churn (until firm).

Serve with fresh raspberries or strawberries.

Makes about 1 litre

Ice Creams

Tia Maria and Chocolate

Ingredients

450mL FRESH CREAM
3 drops vanilla essence
1 cup cooking chocolate (grated)
6 egg yolks
100g caster sugar
2 tablespoons Tia Maria
150mL THICKENED CREAM
1 teaspoon orange rind (grated)

Method

1. Heat fresh cream and vanilla, and add half of the grated chocolate. Allow to melt.

2. Whisk egg yolks and sugar together, and pour on chocolate and cream. Beat, and reheat (until thickened). Allow to cool.

3. Add rest of chocolate, Tia Maria, thickened cream and grated orange rind. Pour into ice cream maker and churn until firm. Serve immediately (or turn into container and freeze).

Makes about 1 litre

Butter

The unique qualities of butter have been recognised and used by chefs throughout the years to perfect the flavour, texture and appearance of different foods. Butter, in simple terms, is milkfat separated from the liquid.

Butter—Made Naturally

At the butter factory, milk is separated into cream and skim milk. The cream is pasteurised and cooled. It is then pumped into stainless steel churns in which beaters agitate it. This is known as churning.

The beating makes the milkfat globules combine into larger and larger globules and finally creates what we know as butter. The liquid that is left (buttermilk) is drained away and used for other purposes.

Types of Butter

Buttermilk: This is produced by adding the necessary culture to pasteurised skim milk and allowing this culture to work for 12–14 hours (at 14°C). Buttermilk today is a cultured manufactured product rather than a by-product of butter production. It is very low in fat.

Salted Regular Butter: This is the regular butter. Cream is churned, and about 2 per cent salt is added (after the buttermilk is drained off).

Unsalted Regular Butter: Cream is churned, but no salt is added.

Unsalted Cultured Butter: Also called Danish-style butter. Before churning, a selected culture is added to the cream, which is held (usually overnight) to allow the acid flavour to develop. No salt is added after draining the buttermilk.

Salted Cultured Butter: The Australian preference for a salty taste in butter has brought some changes to the traditional European cultured butter. A small quantity of salt (usually about one per cent) is added to cultured butter (made as described above).

Ghee (clarified butter): Used mainly in cooking, ghee has advantages over butter in some forms of cooking (such as pan frying), as it does not begin to smoke or brown until it reaches a very high temperature.

Sweet Red Capsicum Soup

Ingredients

4 large red capsicums
30g BUTTER
1 leek (sliced and washed)
1 clove garlic (crushed)
1 x 440g can peeled tomatoes (undrained, chopped)
2 cups vegetable stock
½ cup LIGHT SOUR CREAM
salt and pepper (to taste)
¼ cup LIGHT SOUR CREAM (extra)
1 tablespoon chives (snipped)

Method

1. Bake the whole capsicums (at 200°C) for 20 minutes (or until the skins have blistered). Place in a paper bag and allow to cool before removing skin and seeds.
2. Melt the butter in a saucepan, and sauté the leek and garlic for 5 minutes.
3. Add the tomatoes, capsicums and stock, and bring to the boil. Simmer covered for 15 minutes (or until vegetables are soft).
4. Drain the vegetables (reserving the liquid) and purée in a food processor (until smooth). Gradually add the liquid, puréeing continuously (until blended).
5. Return to a clean saucepan, add the sour cream and chives, and season to taste. Reheat (without boiling), and serve with a swirl of extra sour cream.

Serves 4

Reduced Fat Spreads

These are a mixture in which the fat content is 30–60 per cent of the total product. A reduced fat dairy spread contains milkfat and milk protein (as opposed to vegetable oils and fats). The reduced fat spread products, of dairy or margarine, contain half the fat of regular table spreads. To make sure that the table spread you choose retains that great 'buttery' taste, look for the words 'butter' or 'dairy', which guarantee that a major component of the product comes from pure, natural dairy ingredients.

Spinach Blinis with Tomato Chive Butter

Ingredients

½ cup MILK
7g sachet dried yeast
2 teaspoons caster sugar
¾ cup wholemeal flour
1 egg (separated)
40g BUTTER (melted)
125g frozen spinach (thawed and well drained)
125g UNSALTED BUTTER
1 tablespoon tomato paste
1 teaspoon Worcestershire sauce
1 tablespoon chives (snipped)
6 cherry tomatoes (halved)

Makes 12

Method

1. Bring milk to the boil and allow to cool (until lukewarm). Stir in yeast and sugar, cover and stand in a warm place (until frothy).

2. Stir the flour, egg yolk, melted butter and spinach together (until well combined). Add the yeast mixture, cover and stand (until almost doubled).

3. Beat the egg whites (until stiff peaks form) and fold into the batter. In a buttered frying pan cook 1 teaspoonful of the mixture (until brown on both sides).

4. Cream the unsalted butter, tomato paste, Worcestershire sauce and chives (until smooth). Pipe on top of blinis and garnish with cherry tomato halves.

Curried Seafood in Shells

Curried Seafood in Shells

(photographed above)

Ingredients

100g BUTTER
2 spring onions (chopped)
½ red capsicum (chopped)
1 clove garlic (crushed)
3 teaspoons curry powder
2 teaspoons lemon juice
1 tablespoon chopped coriander
750g assorted seafood (scallops, oysters, mussels)
scallop shells (for serving)

Method

1. Melt the butter in a saucepan and sauté the spring onions, red capsicum, garlic and curry together (until softened). Remove from heat and stir in the lemon juice and coriander.

2. Arrange the seafood in the scallop shells on an oven tray.

3. Spoon the curry butter over each piece of seafood and grill until golden brown. Serve immediately.

Serves 6

Butter Parslied Chicken

Ingredients

125g BUTTER
4 large chicken breasts
½ cup plain flour
salt and pepper
1 tablespoon lemon juice
3 tablespoons fresh parsley (chopped)

Method

1. Melt butter in a heavy-based frypan (until foaming subsides). Season flour with salt and pepper and toss in chicken breasts.

2. Sauté chicken breasts in pan for 3 minutes, then turn and cook for a further 2–3 minutes (or until the juices run clear when pierced with a skewer).

3. Remove chicken, leaving butter in the pan. Increase heat (until butter turns a very light nut-brown). Add the lemon juice and parsley. Spoon over the chicken

4. Serve with vegetables such as sautéed potatoes, buttered whole beans and stuffed tomatoes.

Serves 4

Chilli Beef Pappadams with Mint Raita

Ingredients
20g GHEE
1 onion (chopped)
1 teaspoon red chilli (chopped)
1 teaspoon cumin (ground)
pinch cinnamon
250g beef mince
2 tablespoons tomato paste
2 teaspoons cornflour
12 large pappadams
GHEE (for shallow frying)
1 cup NATURAL YOGURT
½ cucumber (seeded and chopped)
2 tablespoons mint (chopped)

Serves 4

Method

1. Melt the ghee in a frying pan and sauté the onion, chilli, cumin, cinnamon, mince and tomato paste (until well browned).
2. Mix the cornflour to a paste with a little water. Dip the pappadams in water to soften. Drain on absorbent paper.
3. Place a tablespoon of filling in the centre of each pappadam, brush the edges with cornflour paste and fold in half to enclose filling.
4. Heat the ghee in a frying pan and fry the pappadams (until golden). Drain on absorbent paper.
5. Combine the yogurt, cucumber and mint together and serve as a sauce with the pappadams.

Filled Fish Cutlets with Chilli Yogurt Salsa

(photographed above)

Ingredients

30g BUTTER
4 spring onions (chopped)
½ red capsicum (chopped)
2 rashers lean bacon (chopped)
1 cup fresh white breadcrumbs
½ cup grated CHEDDAR CHEESE
2 teaspoons Worcestershire sauce
salt and pepper (to taste)
4 trevally or blue eye cutlets
1 tablespoon lemon juice
1 teaspoon Worcestershire sauce (extra)
1 cup NATURAL YOGURT
½–1 teaspoon fresh chilli (chopped)
1 tablespoon fresh chives (snipped)
1 tablespoon lemon juice (extra)

Method

1. Melt the butter in a frypan. Add half of the spring onions, half of the red capsicum and all of the bacon, and sauté for 5 minutes.
2. Add the breadcrumbs, cheese and Worcestershire sauce to form a seasoning. Season with salt and pepper to taste.
3. Press the seasoning into the centre cavity of each fish cutlet. Brush with lemon juice and extra Worcestershire sauce and grill for 4–5 minutes on each side (or until cooked through).
4. Combine the remaining ingredients with the remaining red capsicum and spring onion, and serve with the fish and tossed salad.

Serves 4

Spicy Lamb Steaks with Asparagus

(photographed below)

Ingredients

4 trim lamb leg steaks
garlic salt (for sprinkling)
dried thyme or oregano (for sprinkling)
paprika (for sprinkling)
20g BUTTER
8 asparagus spears (cooked)
¼ cup white wine
¼ cup tomato sauce
1 tablespoon French mustard
½ cup CRÈME FRAÎCHE or LIGHT SOUR CREAM
seasonal vegetables, for serving

Method

1. Sprinkle the lamb steaks with garlic salt, thyme and paprika on both sides.
2. Melt the butter in a frypan and cook the steaks for 5–7 minutes on each side (or until done to your liking). Remove the steaks, top with 2 asparagus spears and keep warm.
3. Add the wine, tomato sauce and mustard to the pan and bring to the boil, stirring until combined. Remove from heat and whisk in the crème fraîche.
4. Pour the sauce over the steaks and serve with seasonal vegetables.

Serves 4

Creole Chicken with Tomato Salsa

Creole Chicken with Tomato Salsa

(photographed above)

Ingredients

125g BUTTER
1 teaspoon freshly ground pepper
½ teaspoon cayenne pepper
1 tablespoon ground thyme
¼ teaspoon salt
¼ cup lemon juice
2 tomatoes, diced
½ cucumber (seeded and diced)
2 spring onions (chopped)
French dressing (to taste)
6 chicken fillets (skinned)

Method

1. Melt the butter and whisk in the spices and lemon juice. Allow to cool until thickened.
2. Combine the tomato, cucumber and spring onions together and moisten with French dressing. Allow to stand until required.
3. Spread each chicken fillet with the creole butter and pan fry, BBQ or chargrill (until cooked to your liking). Serve with tomato salsa.

Serves 6

Cottage Beef Steaks

Ingredients

20g BUTTER
1 onion (grated)
½ cup carrot (grated)
½ cup zucchini (grated)
1 tablespoon sesame seeds (toasted)
200g COTTAGE CHEESE
4 beef fillet or lean scotch fillet steaks
1 tablespoon lemon juice
1 tablespoon honey
1 tablespoon light soy sauce
toasted sesame seeds (for garnish)
snow peas, potatoes and pumpkin (cooked, for serving)

Method

1. Melt the butter in a frypan and sauté the onion, carrot and zucchini (until softened and all liquid has evaporated). Allow to cool and add the sesame seeds and cottage cheese.
2. Cut a deep pocket into the side of each steak and fill with half of the cheese mixture. Secure with skewers.
3. Combine the lemon juice, honey and soy, and brush over the steaks. Grill or pan fry (for 5 minutes on each side) basting occasionally.
4. Top with remaining cottage mixture. Sprinkle with sesame seeds and serve with snow peas, potatoes and pumpkin.

Serves 4

Creamy Summer Fettucine

(photographed at right)

Ingredients

250g egg fettucine
150g spinach fettucine
30g BUTTER
4 spring onions (chopped)
2 rashers lean bacon (sliced)
1 punnet cherry tomatoes (halved)
1 avocado (diced)
¾ cup REDUCED CREAM
½ cup PARMESAN CHEESE (grated)
2 teaspoons tomato paste

Method

1. Cook the fettucine in a saucepan of boiling water for 10–15 minutes or until 'al dente'. Drain and keep warm.
2. Melt the butter and sauté the spring onions and bacon for 2–3 minutes. Add the remaining ingredients and heat gently without boiling. Add the fettuccine and toss (until well combined).
3. Serve immediately sprinkled with extra Parmesan cheese.

Serves 6

Vegetable Mélange with Havarti Cashew Sauce

Ingredients

2 large carrots (peeled and sliced diagonally)
2 zucchini (sliced diagonally)
½ cauliflower (cut into small florets)
200g snow peas (tailed)
30g BUTTER
2 tablespoons plain flour
2 cups SKIM MILK
1¼ cup HAVARTI CHEESE (grated)
¼ cup cashew nuts (roasted unsalted)

Method

1. Blanch the vegetables separately in a large saucepan of boiling water for 2–3 minutes (or until just tender). Drain and place in an ovenproof dish.
2. Melt the butter in a saucepan. Add the flour and cook, stirring for 1 minute. Add the milk and cook (until slightly thickened) stirring occasionally. Add 1 cup of cheese and the cashews and stir (until melted).
3. Pour over the vegetables and sprinkle with remaining cheese. Grill for 5 minutes, or bake at 200°C for 15 minutes (until heated through).

Serves 6

Jan's Handy Tip

Beurre Manie: An uncooked paste of equal amounts of butter and flour. Used to build up sauces that are too thin. To make Beurre Manie, knead butter and flour together with fingers, or mash with a fork.

For soup use 1 tablespoon flour and 1 tablespoon butter to thicken 1 cup of liquid.

For a sauce use double the quantity to thicken 1 cup of liquid. Extra Beurre Manie may be stored, wrapped in GLAD Wrap, in the refrigerator for about 10 days.

Chicken Breasts in Green Peppercorn Sauce

Ingredients

60g BUTTER
juice of 1 lemon
salt and pepper (to taste)
4 chicken breasts (trimmed)
1 tablespoon flour
2 tablespoons canned green peppercorns (strained)
2 slices shoulder ham (cut into fine strips)
¾ cup SOUR CREAM
strips of ham (for garnish)
steamed zucchini wedges (for serving)

Method

1. Melt butter in a pan over a medium heat. When bubbling, add lemon juice, salt and pepper.
2. Fry chicken breasts gently on both sides, remove from pan, and keep warm.
3. To the cooking juices, add the flour and cook, stirring continuously (until thick and smooth).
4. Add peppercorns and ham and gently cook over a low heat. Blend in sour cream and re-heat without boiling.
5. Spoon sauce over chicken, garnish with strips of ham and serve with steamed zucchini wedges.

Serves 4

Sun-dried Tomato, Olive and Garlic Bread

(photographed page 67)

Ingredients

3 cloves garlic (crushed)
½ cup black olives (pitted and chopped)
1 teaspoon oregano (dried)
¼ cup sun-dried tomatoes (chopped)
125g BUTTER (softened)
1 French bread stick

Method

1. Blend garlic, olives, herbs and sun-dried tomatoes in a food processor (until finely chopped). Add butter and blend (until smooth).
2. Cut the French stick into 2-cm slices (to within 5mm of the base). Spread the butter on each side of the slices.
3. Wrap in foil and bake (at 200°C) for 15–20 minutes. Serve hot.

Serves 4

Sun-dried Tomato, Olive and Garlic Bread (recipe page 66)

Basil-buttered Beef with Matchstick Vegetables

(photographed below)

Ingredients

125g BUTTER (softened)
1 tablespoon French mustard
½ cup basil or parsley (finely chopped)
1 clove garlic (crushed)
1 tablespoon green peppercorns (crushed)
1kg piece beef fillet or porterhouse (trimmed)
1 large carrot (cut into matchstick strips)
1 large zucchini (cut into matchstick strips)
1 red capsicum (cut into matchstick strips)

Method

1. Combine the butter, mustard, basil, garlic and green peppercorns together. Roll half of the butter mixture into a log shape, wrap in foil, and refrigerate.
2. Spread the remaining butter mixture over the beef and bake (at 200°C) for 30 minutes for medium (or until done to your liking). Allow to rest for 10 minutes.
3. Blanch the vegetables in boiling water for 1 minute, and drain.
4. Carve the beef into thick slices. Serve each slice topped with matchstick vegetables and a slice of basil butter.

Serves 8

Jan's Handy Tip

To enhance the natural sweetness of root vegetables, such as carrots, parsnips, onions or turnips, add a pinch of sugar or a few drops of orange juice while cooking.

Pizza Loaf

Ingredients

30g BUTTER (cubed)
2 cups self-raising flour
¾ cup MILK
2 tablespoons tomato paste
½ onion (sliced)
100g salami (cut into strips)
½ red capsicum (chopped)
100g button mushrooms (sliced)
1½ cups MOZZARELLA CHEESE (grated)
1 teaspoon oregano
1 tablespoon MILK (extra)

Method

1. Rub the butter into the flour (until the mixture resembles breadcrumbs). Mix in the milk to form a dough. Knead lightly and roll out to a rectangle 30cm x 40cm.
2. Spread with tomato paste and layer with onion, salami, capsicum, mushrooms and cheese. Sprinkle with oregano and roll up (as for a Swiss roll).
3. Using scissors, make deep cuts three quarters of the way through the top of the roll at 3cm intervals, ensuring not to cut all the way through.
4. Place on an oven tray and brush with extra milk. Bake (at 220°C) for 20 minutes (or until golden brown).

Serves 6

Jan's Handy Tip

Try substituting reduced fat Mozzarella and low fat milk, for a lower kilojoule count in this recipe.

Basil Buttered Beef with Matchstick Vegetables

Peach and Passionfruit Crumble Pie

Peach and Passionfruit Crumble Pie

(photographed above)

Ingredients

1⅓ cups plain flour
pinch baking powder
100g BUTTER (cubed)
1 egg
¼ cup caster sugar
2 x 425g cans peach pie filling
¼ cup cornflour
¼ cup passionfruit pulp
¼ cup almonds (flaked)

Method

1. Place the flour and baking powder in a food processor. Add the butter and blend (until evenly distributed).
2. Combine the egg and sugar together, and add to the flour mixture. Blend until the mixture forms a ball.
3. Roll out three quarters of the mixture to line a 25cm flan tin with removable base. Refrigerate for 10 minutes.
4. Line with GLAD Bake and load with rice or beans. Blind bake (at 200°C) for 15 minutes. Remove the rice or beans and bake (at 180°C) for a further 10 minutes.
5. Combine the peach, cornflour and passionfruit together, and place into the pastry case. Grate the remaining pastry over the surface, and sprinkle with almonds.
6. Bake (at 200°C) for 20–30 minutes (or until the pastry is golden). Allow to cool. Serve cut into wedges.

Serves 12

Fresh Fruit and Coconut Shortcake

Ingredients

2 cups wholemeal self-raising flour
1 cup coconut (desiccated)
3 teaspoons mixed spice
125g BUTTER (melted)
½ cup honey
1 cup MILK
selection of fresh fruit (apricots, kiwifruit, peaches, raspberries)
1 cup clear apple juice
3 teaspoons agar-agar powder (or gelatine)
1 tablespoon honey
CREAM (whipped, for serving)

Method

1. Combine the flour, coconut and mixed spices in a bowl. Make a well in the centre, and mix in the butter, honey and milk (to make a cake batter).
2. Place into a buttered deep (22cm x 28cm) lamington tin. Bake (at 190°C) for 20–25 minutes (or until golden brown). Allow to cool in the tin.
3. Arrange the fruit decoratively over the cake base.
4. Combine the apple juice, agar-agar powder (or gelatine) and honey in a saucepan and bring to the boil (until the agar-agar powder dissolves). Allow to cool and refrigerate (until semi-set) before pouring over fruit. Refrigerate (until set).
5. Cut into wedges and serve with whipped cream.

Note: Agar-agar powder is also known as Kanton, and is a setting agent derived from a sea vegetable. It is a suitable substitute for gelatine, which is an animal derivative and therefore not regarded as a vegetarian product.

Serves 10

Walnut and Date Muffins

Walnut and Date Muffins

(photographed above)

Ingredients

125g UNSALTED BUTTER
1 cup brown sugar
1 egg (lightly beaten)
¾ cup dates (chopped, dried)
½ cup walnuts (chopped)
2 cups plain flour (sifted)
1 teaspoon bicarbonate of soda
1½ cups BUTTERMILK
walnuts (chopped, for garnish)

Method

1. Cream the butter and sugar together (until light and fluffy). Gradually beat in the egg. Fold through the remaining ingredients and mix well.
2. Spoon into 12 buttered muffin tins, and garnish with walnuts.
3. Bake (at 180°C) for 25–30 minutes (or until golden brown).

Makes 12

Apricot Cottage Muffins

Ingredients

125g BUTTER
1 cup brown sugar
1 egg (lightly beaten)
300g COTTAGE CHEESE
1 cup apricots (chopped, dried)
2 cups plain flour (sifted)
1 teaspoon bicarbonate of soda
½ cup MILK

Method

1. Cream the butter and sugar together (until light and fluffy). Gradually beat in the egg.
2. Fold through the remaining ingredients, and mix well.
3. Spoon into 12 buttered muffin tins and bake (at 180°C) for 25–30 minutes (or until golden brown).

Makes 12

Nutty Cookies

Ingredients

60g BUTTER
1 tablespoon golden syrup
½ teaspoon bicarbonate of soda
2 tablespoons water (boiling)
1 cup muesli (toasted)
1 cup flour
¼ cup instant REGULAR MILK POWDER
½ cup brown sugar
½ cup dates (chopped)
⅓ cup nuts (chopped)

Method

1. Melt the butter and golden syrup together in a small pan.
2. Mix together the bicarbonate of soda and boiling water, pour into the butter mixture, and mix well.
3. Place the remaining ingredients in a bowl, and add the liquid.
4. Mix well, then shape into walnut-sized balls.
5. Place onto a buttered baking tray and bake (at 180°C) for 10 minutes (or until firm to touch). Cool on a wire rack.

Makes 20–24

Sultana Cookies

(photographed below)

Ingredients

125g BUTTER
3 tablespoons golden syrup
½ cup caster sugar
1½ cups rolled oats
¼ cup sultanas
1 cup self-raising flour
1 teaspoon cinnamon
1 egg (lightly beaten)

Method

1. Melt butter and golden syrup together in a medium-sized saucepan. Add sugar and stir (until dissolved).
2. Remove from heat, and stir in oats, sultanas, flour, egg and cinnamon.
3. Place tablespoons of the mixture onto buttered baking trays and flatten slightly. Bake (at 180°C) for 10 minutes.
4. Allow cookies to cool for a few minutes on the tray, and then remove to a wire cooling rack.

Makes 24

Sultana Cookies

Muesli Cookies with Cocoa Cream

(photographed at right)

Ingredients

125g UNSALTED BUTTER
¼ cup raw sugar
¼ cup treacle or golden syrup
1 egg
1 cup self-raising flour
1 cup muesli (natural)
300g CREAM CHEESE (softened)
¾ cup icing sugar
1 tablespoon cocoa
1 teaspoon vanilla essence

Method

1. Cream butter and sugar together (until smooth and creamy). Beat in treacle and egg. Stir in flour and muesli (until well combined).
2. Place heaped teaspoons of the mixture (5cm apart) on a lightly buttered baking tray.
4. Bake (at 160°C) for 20 minutes. Cool on a wire cake-cooler.
5. Beat the cream cheese, sugar, cocoa and vanilla essence together (until combined).
6. Sandwich biscuits together with cocoa cream (just prior to serving).

Makes 18

Rum Omelette Flambé

Ingredients

4 eggs (separated)
4 tablespoons caster sugar
1 tablespoon UNSALTED BUTTER
vanilla ice cream (for serving)

Sauce:

125g UNSALTED BUTTER
2 tablespoons caster sugar
grated rind of 1 orange
¼ cup rum

Method

1. Preheat grill to a moderate setting. Beat egg yolks and 2 tablespoons of the sugar (until pale and creamy).
2. Whisk egg whites (until stiff) adding remaining 2 tablespoons sugar. Fold egg whites gently through yolks. Melt butter in a 20cm omelette pan.
3. Pour in the mixture and cook over medium heat (for 5–7 minutes) lifting the side with a spatula to check when the base is golden brown.
4. Place omelette in the pan under the grill for several minutes (until top is firm and golden). Immediately fold in half and turn into a warm serving dish.
5. Pour flaming sauce (see below) over omelette. Serve with vanilla ice cream.
6. **Sauce:** Melt butter with sugar and orange rind (until sugar has dissolved). Add rum and heat well. Ignite and pour over omelette.

Serves 4

Apple Meringue Pie

Ingredients

Pastry:

1 cup flour
1 tablespoon icing sugar
¼ teaspoon baking powder
¼ teaspoon salt
60g BUTTER
1 tablespoon water

Filling:

4 cooking apples (finely sliced)
1 tablespoon cornflour
1 tablespoon caster sugar
⅓ cup apricots (chopped, dried)

Topping:

2 egg whites
⅓ cup caster sugar
1 tablespoon coconut (desiccated)

Method

1. **Pastry:** Sift together the dry ingredients, and rub in the butter. Mix to a stiff dough with the water.
2. Roll the pastry out thinly. Place into the base of a 21cm buttered pie-dish.
3. **Filling:** Combine the filling ingredients together in a bowl, lightly coating the apples with the flour. Place the filling into the pie-base.
4. **Topping:** Beat the egg whites (until stiff). Add the sugar and beat (until smooth). Fold in the coconut, then spread the topping over the apples and bake (at 190°C) for 45 minutes.

Serve hot or cold.

Serves 6

Honey Macadamia Shortbreads

Ingredients

½ cup unsalted macadamia nuts
1 cup plain flour
½ cup cornflour
¼ teaspoon salt
¼ cup caster sugar
125g UNSALTED BUTTER
2 tablespoons honey

Method

1. Finely chop half of the macadamias. Halve the remainder, and reserve.
2. Sift flour, salt and sugar together. Rub in the butter (until evenly dispersed), and stir in the honey and the half quantity chopped and quarter quantity unchopped macadamia nuts.
3. Turn onto a lightly floured board and knead lightly. Roll out to 1cm-thickness, and refrigerate for 10 minutes before cutting into rounds (using a 4cm-fluted cutter). Place half a nut on each round.
4. Bake (at 200°C) on a baking tray lined with GLAD Bake for 15 minutes (or until golden brown).

Note: Almonds, walnuts or pecan nuts may be substituted for macadamias.

Makes 24

Cream

Cream is a traditional luxury, much prized for its natural richness. For all of recorded history it has been treasured, and has even been absorbed into our language as meaning 'the best of everything'. Fresh cream gives a quality to food that no other product can give.

Cream is the fat component of milk. Cream is formed naturally when the light fat globules rise to the top of unhomogenised milk. When the cream is skimmed off, it leaves skim milk.

From the earliest times, cream was made by allowing milk to settle in large earthenware bowls and then skimming the cream from the surface. Since the beginning of this century, cream has been removed with a separator, which spins the milk and concentrates the cream through density differences. In making cream, there are no chemicals or additives included.

There is no such thing as an average or typical cream. There is a series of creams with varying fat contents suitable for different cooking applications.

Cream adds a natural refinement to dishes and is a versatile flavour-enhancer, perfect for sweet or savoury dishes.

Cream can play a part in a balanced diet

Nutritionists say small amounts of cream and butter can be included in a sensible, balanced diet that contains a wide variety of foods. As well as contributing its own unique taste and texture, cream makes a wide range of foods more palatable. Because it is rich, satisfying and tasty, you need only small portions.

Cream provides high energy value and easily digested simple fats and, when eaten in moderation, can be included in a balanced diet.

Types of Cream

There are many types of cream. Creams are categorised according to their milkfat content.

Rich Cream: 48 per cent milkfat. This is thick enough to be spooned directly from the tub or it may be whipped, and is also referred to as 'double' cream. Use over fruit, for home-made ice cream, mousses and in sweet and savoury sauces, soups and casseroles.

Pure and Whipping Cream: 35 per cent milkfat. Ideal for whipping, it can be used in cakes, pie fillings, soufflés, mousses and cheesecakes. It can also be folded through fruit purées, or used with chilled, fresh or frozen fruit, and is also ideal for cocktails.

Thickened Cream: 35 per cent milkfat. Uses as for pure and whipping cream.

Reduced Cream: 25 per cent milkfat. Usually canned, reduced cream has a shelf life of three months while the can is sealed. It can be used to enrich cocoa, coffee or iced drinks, in custards and sauces, in meat dishes and soups, and as shortening or liquid in cakes and other baked goods. It is also available in sour cream style and in long-life packs.

Light Cream: 18 per cent milkfat. A pouring cream for fruit and pies, and ideal for drinks.

Extra Light Cream: 12 per cent milkfat. Use as for light cream.

Scalded or Clotted Cream: 48 per cent milkfat. It has a thick texture and rich flavour, and is excellent for Devonshire teas. It keeps for 10–12 days.

Crème Fraîche: 48 per cent milkfat. This is a blend of pure and sour cream. A rich, stable cream, it is perfect for reducing for use in sauces, casseroles and soups. It has become very popular in recent years.

Sour Cream: 35 per cent milkfat. Sour cream is a cream that has had selected cultures added to produce a 'tart' flavour. Sour cream is available ready-made and also in reduced-fat or 'light' form with 18 per cent milkfat. It can be used in casseroles and even European-style cakes requiring a 'tart' flavour.

Pressure Pack Cream: 25 per cent milkfat. Available from dairy cabinets, it contains a harmless gas propellant and is a convenient form of ready-whipped cream for serving on desserts.

Long-life (UHT) Cream: 25–35 per cent milkfat. Ultra Heat Treated cream (heated at high temperature for a short period), commonly known as 'long-life', is excellent for pantry storage and travel, but it should be treated like fresh cream after being opened.

Tips on Using Cream

- **Adding to hot liquids**

Care should be taken to avoid cream curdling when adding to hot dishes such as soups, casseroles, hot meats or vegetable dishes. Heat the cream by combining with a little of the hot liquid before stirring-in, and do not boil once added.

- **Reducing for sauces**

Cream may be reduced for use in sauces by rapidly boiling until quantity is reduced by one third.

- **Whipping**

Cream should double in volume on whipping. Best results are achieved at 5°C, which is just above refrigerator temperature. Add flavourings and sugar after cream is whipped. To whip reduced (25 per cent milkfat) cream add 1 teaspoon of lemon juice a few minutes before whipping.

Stilton Soup

Ingredients

50g BUTTER
1 onion (skinned and finely chopped)
2 celery sticks (cleaned and sliced)
40g flour
45mL dry white wine
900mL chicken stock
300mL MILK
100g BLUE STILTON CHEESE (crumbled)
50g CHEDDAR CHEESE (grated)
salt and freshly ground pepper
60mL FRESH DOUBLE CREAM
croûtons (to garnish)

Method

1. Melt the butter in a saucepan, add the vegetables, and fry gently for 5 minutes. Stir in the flour and cook for 1 minute. Remove from the heat, stir in the wine and stock, return to the heat, bring to the boil, and simmer for 30 minutes.
2. Add the milk and cheeses, stirring constantly, and season with salt and pepper. Stir in the fresh cream.
3. Rub through a sieve (or purée in a blender) and reheat without boiling. Serve garnished with croûtons.

Serves 4–6

Oysters Greta Garbo

(photographed below)

Ingredients

3 dozen natural oysters in shells
juice of ½ lime (or lemon)
6 slices smoked salmon (cut into fine strips)
1 cup SOUR CREAM
2 tablespoons chives (snipped)
red caviar (for garnish)
crushed ice (for serving)

Method

1. Sprinkle the oysters with lime juice, and top with smoked salmon.
2. Dollop the sour cream onto each oyster.
3. Garnish with chives and red caviar. Serve on a bed of ice.

Serves 6 (as an entrée)

Jan's Handy Tip

Cream can be frozen, and 48 per cent milkfat cream can be frozen for up to 3 months. Sometimes the fat and liquid tend to separate on thawing, but a light whipping will redisperse the fat and restore smoothness.

Cream under 40 per cent milkfat is best whipped lightly, then frozen for up to 2 months. Ideal storage is in small containers or ice cube trays. Always thaw frozen cream in the refrigerator. Avoid using microwave ovens to thaw cream.

Oysters Greta Garbo

Cream of Chicken Soup

Cream of Chicken Soup

(photographed above)

Ingredients

20g BUTTER
¼ cup plain flour
2 cups chicken stock
1 chicken fillet (skinned)
½ cup RICH CREAM
1 egg yolk
snipped chives (snipped, for garnish)
50 GHEE or BUTTER
4 slices of bread (cut into shapes)

Method

1. Melt the butter in a large saucepan, add the flour, and cook (stirring) for 1 minute. Add the stock, and heat (stirring, until thickened).
2. Add the chicken and simmer (covered) for 15 minutes. Remove the chicken and finely dice.
3. Blend the cream and egg yolk together. Whisk a little of the hot stock into the cream, and then add the cream mixture to the remaining stock.
4. Add the chicken, and reheat gently (without boiling).
5. To make the croûtons, heat the ghee and fry the bread shapes (until golden). Drain on absorbent paper.
6. Serve soup garnished with chives and croûtons.

Serves 4

Seafood and Apple Scallops

Ingredients

3 tablespoons BUTTER
½ bunch spring onions (trimmed and chopped finely)
1 medium-sized cooking apple (cored and cut into 1cm dice)
2 teaspoons mild curry powder
1 tablespoon plain flour
1 cup apple juice
1 bay leaf
1 teaspoon salt
500g scallops
8 prawns (peeled and deveined)
1 medium banana (sliced)
½ cup REDUCED CREAM
cooked rice (for serving)

Method

1. Melt the butter in a saucepan. Add spring onions and apple, and sauté for 5 minutes.
2. Add curry powder, and cook for 1 minute. Remove from heat. Blend in flour, then apple juice.
3. Return to heat. Bring to boil (stirring constantly). Add bay leaf and salt. Simmer for 5 minutes.
4. Stir in scallops, prawns and bananas. Cook until just tender.
5. Add cream, and heat through gently (without boiling). Accompany with rice.

Serves 4

Confetti Spaghetti with Bacon Cream Sauce

(photographed below)

Ingredients

2 rashers bacon (lean, finely sliced)
2 spring onions (sliced)
1 clove garlic (crushed)
1 tablespoon tomato paste
1 cup THICKENED CREAM
¼ cup PARMESAN CHEESE (grated)
15g BUTTER
1 leek (thinly sliced)
1 carrot (grated)
1 zucchini (grated)
1 red capsicum (cut into fine strips)
500g spaghetti (cooked)

Method

1. Cook the bacon, spring onions and garlic in a non-stick frypan (until softened). Add the tomato paste, cream and cheese, and simmer (until heated through). Keep sauce warm.
2. Melt the butter in a large saucepan and sauté the leek, carrot, zuchhini and red capsicum (until softened). Add the hot spaghetti and toss to combine.
3. Serve spaghetti with bacon cream sauce.

Serves 4

Parmesan Egg Ramekins

Ingredients

approximately 250g eggplant (cut into slices)
salt and black pepper (to taste)
3 tablespoons BUTTER
½ cup PARMESAN CHEESE (grated)
6 x 8cm slices mortadella sausage (cut into strips)
½ cup THICKENED CREAM
½ teaspoon Italian seasoning
6 eggs
tossed tomato and artichoke salad (for serving)
hot crusty French bread (for serving)

Method

1. Season eggplant with salt and pepper. Melt butter in a frying pan. Add eggplant, and sauté for 1–2 minutes. Remove and drain on absorbent paper.
2. Butter 6 deep (8cm-round) ovenproof dishes with remaining butter from pan. Arrange eggplant slices on the base of each dish.
3. Sprinkle half of the Parmesan cheese over the eggplant slices. Cover completely with mortadella strips.
4. Combine cream, Italian seasoning and remaining Parmesan cheese. Season with salt and pepper. Spoon into each dish. Carefully break an egg on top of each.
5. Place dishes in a pan of simmering water. Bake (at 190°C) for 15 minutes. Leave standing in the pan for 5–10 minutes (until edges are lightly set). Serve immediately with tossed tomato and artichoke salad, and hot crusty French bread.

Serves 6

Confetti Spaghetti with Bacon Cream Sauce

Duo of Carrot and Pea Soups

Ingredients

¼ cup light sour cream (for serving)
sprigs of fresh mint (for serving)

Carrot Soup:

20g BUTTER
1 onion (diced)
500g carrots (peeled and diced)
2½ cups chicken stock
1 tablespoon finely chopped fresh mint
½ cup LIGHT SOUR CREAM

Pea Soup:

20g BUTTER
1 onion (diced)
500g peas (frozen)
1½ cups chicken stock
1 tablespoon chives (fresh, finely chopped)
¼ cup LIGHT SOUR CREAM

Method

1. **Carrot Soup:** Melt the butter in a saucepan and sauté the onion and carrots for 5 minutes. Add the stock and simmer covered for 15 minutes (until tender).
2. Purée and return to a clean saucepan. Add the mint and sour cream and season with salt and pepper (to taste). Reheat without boiling.
3. **Pea Soup:** Proceed as for carrot soup, substituting ingredients for pea soup.
4. **To Serve:** Place each hot soup into a jug and pour simultaneously into warm serving bowls to achieve a two-tone effect. Serve with a swirl of sour cream and sprig of fresh mint.

Serves 4

Fruity Kebabs with Two Sauces

Ingredients

1 punnet strawberries (hulled)
2 large bananas (thickly sliced and sprinkled with lemon juice)
1 mango (cubed)
2 kiwifuit (peeled and cubed)
1 x 440g can pineapple pieces (unsweetened, drained)
½ cup NATURAL YOGURT
1 tablespoon honey
pulp of 1 passionfruit
½ cup REDUCED CREAM
50g choc bits
2 teaspoons liqueur (e.g. Kahlúa)
1 tablespoon almonds (flaked, toasted)
12 bamboo skewers (soaked for 30 minutes)

Method

1. Thread the fruitpieces onto 12 bamboo skewers.
2. Combine the yogurt, honey and passionfruit to form a sauce. Pour the cream into a saucepan, and bring to the boil. Remove from the heat, and stir in choc bits and liqueur (until smooth).
3. Serve yogurt sauce and chocolate sauce with the fruit kebabs. Sprinkle with almonds.

Serves 6

Vegetable Baton Salad with Minted Dressing

Ingredients

1 large beetroot
2 carrots (peeled)
2 zucchini
2 yellow zucchini
1 large red capsicum
1 bunch young asparagus
lemon juice (to taste)
½ cup SOUR CREAM
2 tablespoons mayonnaise
1 teaspoon French mustard
2 tablespoons mint (fresh, finely chopped)
2 tablespoons French dressing

Method

1. Cook the whole beetroot in a saucepan of boiling water for 15–20 minutes (or until fork-tender). Allow to cool before peeling and cutting into finger-length batons (1cm-thick).
2. Cut the remaining vegetables into batons of similar size and blanch each variety separately in boiling water (until just tender). Drain and refresh under cold water. Sprinkle with lemon juice.
3. Combine the remaining ingredients together to form a dressing. (The flavour will develop further on standing.)
4. Arrange the vegetables decoratively on a platter, and drizzle over the dressing just prior to serving.

Serves 8

Orange Apricot Cream

Ingredients

1 x 425g can apricots (in natural juice)
1 teaspoon orange-rind (grated)
½ cup REDUCED CREAM (whipped)
200g APRICOT LOW FAT YOGURT
2 teaspoons agar-agar powder or gelatine (dissolved in 1 tablespoon hot water)
½ cup fresh orange juice (sweetened if desired)
2 teaspoons agar-agar powder or gelatine (extra, dissolved in 1 tablespoon hot water)

Method

1. Drain the apricots and purée (reserving a few pieces to garnish).
2. Combine purée with orange-rind, cream, yogurt and agar-agar powder (or gelatine). Spoon the mixture into 4 parfait glasses and refrigerate until set.
3. Combine the orange juice and extra agar-agar powder (or gelatine) and pour over the apricot cream. Refrigerate until set.
3. Serve with reserved fruit.

Note: Agar-agar powder is also known as Kanton, and is a setting agent derived from a sea vegetable. It is a suitable substitute for gelatine, which is an animal derivative and therefore not regarded as a vegetarian product.

Serves 4

Chicken and Mushroom Enchiladas

Ingredients
2⅔ cups wholemeal flour
1 teaspoon salt
40g BUTTER
1¼ cups hot water
3 cooked chicken fillets (diced)
125g button mushrooms (sliced)
3 spring onions (chopped)
1 clove garlic (crushed)
1½ cups LIGHT SOUR CREAM
½ cup CHEDDAR CHEESE (grated)
1 x 200mL jar taco sauce

Method
1. Combine flour and salt together. Rub in butter and mix in hot water to form a dough. Knead until smooth.
2. Divide into 12 pieces and roll each piece out thinly into a tortilla (20cm in diameter). Heat a non-stick frying pan and cook each tortilla for 30 seconds on each side (until golden).
3. Combine chicken, mushrooms, spring onions, garlic, 1 cup sour cream and half the cheese together. Place the mixture into the centre of each tortilla and fold in the sides.
4. Place in a baking dish, pour the taco sauce over the tortillas, and sprinkle with remaining cheese. Bake (at 180°C) for 20 minutes (or until heated through).
5. Serve topped with remaining sour cream.

Serves 6

Sun-dried Tomato and Basil Dip

Sun-dried Tomato and Basil Dip

(photographed at left)

Ingredients

1 clove garlic (crushed)
2 spring onions (chopped)
¼ cup fresh basil
½ cup sun-dried tomatoes
1 tablespoon tomato paste
200g CREAM CHEESE (softened)
½ cup LIGHT SOUR CREAM
pita wedges and vegetable pieces (for serving)

Method

1. Place the garlic, spring onions, basil and sun-dried tomatoes in a food processor and blend (until finely chopped).
2. Mix in the remaining ingredients and refrigerate (until chilled).
3. Serve with pita wedges and vegetable pieces.

Serves 8 (makes 1½ cups)

Hot Lips with Avocado Dip

(photographed below)

Ingredients

4 large Pontiac potatoes
60g BUTTER (melted)
1 clove garlic (crushed)
1 teaspoon mild chilli sauce
paprika (for sprinkling)
garlic salt (for sprinkling)
dried thyme (for sprinkling)
freshly ground black pepper
1 ripe avocado
2 tablespoons chives (snipped)
2 tablespoons lemon juice
1 cup LIGHT SOUR CREAM

Method

1. Wash potatoes and cut into wedges. Brush with combined butter, garlic and chilli sauce. Sprinkle liberally with paprika, garlic salt, thyme and pepper.
2. Bake (at 230°C) for 30 minutes, basting occasionally with butter mixture.
3. Blend remaining ingredients in a food processor (until smooth) and serve with hot lips.

Serves 8

Hot Lips with Avocado Dip

Mushroom and Capsicum Pinwheels

(photographed below)

Ingredients

3 cups self-raising flour (sifted)
1¼ cups CREAM
½ cup SKIM MILK
30g BUTTER
100g mushrooms (sliced)
3 spring onions (chopped)
1 red capsicum (seeded and diced)
1 green capsicum (seeded and diced)
50g TASTY CHEDDAR CHEESE (grated)
¼ cup PARMESAN CHEESE (grated)

Makes 12

Method

1. Place the flour in a large mixing bowl and make a well in the centre. Stir in combined cream and milk to form a dough. Turn out onto a lightly floured board and roll out to form a 10cm x 30cm rectangle.
2. Melt the butter in a frypan and sauté the mushrooms, spring onions and capsicums until softened. Sprinkle the tasty cheese over the scone dough, and top with mushroom mixture. Roll the scone dough into a log shape, and slice into 3cm-rounds.
3. Place on a scone tray lined with GLAD Bake and top with Parmesan cheese. Bake (at 230°C) for 10 minutes, then reduce heat (to 210°C) for 5 minutes (until cooked). Serve hot or cold.

Mushroom and Capsicum Pinwheels

Vegetable Kebabs with Peanut Sauce

(photographed at right)

Ingredients

6 yellow squash
1 green capsicum (deseeded and chopped)
8 cherry tomatoes
8 mushrooms
1 tablespoon light soy sauce
1 tablespoon lemon juice
¼ cup peanut BUTTER
½ cup LIGHT SOUR CREAM
2 teaspoons sweet chilli sauce
cooked brown rice (for serving)
12 bamboo skewers (soaked for 30 minutes)

Method

1. Thread the vegetables alternately onto bamboo skewers that have been soaked in water.
2. Grill for 2–3 minutes on each side, basting with soy and lemon juice. Heat the peanut butter in a saucepan until melted.

Makes 12

Vegetable Kebabs with Peanut Sauce

Veal in Pesto Cream Sauce

(photographed below)

Ingredients

6 veal steaks
freshly ground black pepper (to taste)
15g BUTTER
2 teaspoons cornflour
1 cup PURE CREAM
2 tablespoons pesto sauce
1 tablespoon pine nuts (toasted)
fresh basil (for garnish)

Method

1. Season the veal with pepper. Melt the butter in a frying pan and sauté the veal for 2–3 minutes on each side. Remove from pan and keep warm.
2. Combine the cornflour and cream and add to the pan. Heat until almost boiling. Remove from heat and whisk in pesto and half of the pine nuts.
3. Serve sauce over veal and sprinkle with remaining pine nuts. Garnish with basil.

Note: Pesto Sauce is made from fresh basil, Parmesan cheese, pine nuts and olive oil, and is commercially available in jars.

Serves 4

Mushroom Quiche

Ingredients

175g shortcrust pastry
225g button mushrooms (wiped and thinly sliced)
25g BUTTER
1 egg (plus 1 egg yolk)
150mL FRESH CREAM
½ teaspoon basil (dried)
salt and freshly ground pepper

Method

1. Roll out the pastry and use to line a 21cm-flan dish (or ring) placed on a baking sheet. Bake blind in the oven (at 200°C) for 20 minutes (until set).
2. Sauté the mushrooms gently in the butter for 5 minutes. Drain and place in the flan case.
3. Beat together the egg and yolk, add the cream, basil and seasoning, and pour this over the mushrooms.
4. Bake (at 190° C) for about 35 minutes (until just set).

Serves 4–6

Jan's Handy Tip

Too much liquid cream can make dishes taste bland. Always test for flavour as it is added to your cooking.

Veal in Pesto Cream Sauce

Salmon and Mustard Cream

(photographed below)

Ingredients

1 cup CREAM
2 tablespoons wholegrain mustard
4 salmon cutlets

Method

1. Place cream in a large bowl. Microwave on HIgh (100%) for 8 minutes (or until reduced to one third). Stir in mustard.
2. Place fish on a plate, cover with GLAD Microwave Wrap and cook for 2 minutes. Stand for a few minutes.
3. Reheat sauce (if necessary) and serve over the fish.

Serves 4

Jan's Handy Tip

Cream will keep 7–10 days under refrigeration, but be guided by the 'use-by' date. Always keep tightly covered, as it absorbs other flavours easily. Once a can of reduced cream or pack of longlife cream is opened, it should be treated as normal cream. Sour cream can generally be stored in the refrigerator for up to 15 days.

Trout in Cream

Ingredients

4 trout
juice of 1 lemon
1 tablespoon chives (fresh, chopped)
1 tablespoon parsley (fresh, chopped)
150mL FRESH CREAM
2 level tablespoons breadcrumbs (fresh)
a little BUTTER (melted)

Method

1. Clean the fish, leaving the heads on (if you wish). Wash and wipe the fish, lay them in a buttered shallow flameproof dish.
2. Sprinkle the lemon juice, herbs and about 1 tablespoon water over the fish. Cover with OSO Aluminium Foil.
3. Cook in the oven (at 180°C) for 10–15 minutes, until tender.
4. Heat the cream gently and pour over the fish. Sprinkle with breadcrumbs and melted butter, and brown under a hot grill. Serve immediately.

Serves 4

Salmon and Mustard Cream

Cinnamon Roulade with Toffeed Walnut Cream

Choc-Orange Ring Cake

Ingredients

125g BUTTER
¾ cup caster sugar
2 eggs
⅓ cup orange marmalade
¾ cup SOUR CREAM
1½ cups self-raising flour (sifted)
¼ cup cocoa (sifted)
melted dark chocolate and mandarin sections

Icing:

2 cups icing sugar (sifted)
½ cup SOUR CREAM
2 tablespoons orange marmalade

Method

1. Cream together the butter and sugar (until light and fluffy).
2. Add the eggs 1 at a time and beat in well. Mix in the marmalade.
3. Add one-third of the sour cream and one-third of the dry ingredients alternately until all are combined.
4. Pour mixture into a buttered and lined 25cm x 7cm ring pan, and cook in a microwave oven on High (100%) for 7½ minutes on a rack.
5. Allow to stand for 5 minutes (directly on bench), then allow to cool on a wire rack.
6. **Icing:** Beat together all ingredients, spread over cake, then decorate with melted dark chocolate and the mandarin sections.

Serves 8–10

Jan's Handy Tip

For early attempts at icing, practise first on an upturned plate using some butter icing, or mashed potato.

Cinnamon Roulade with Toffeed Walnut Cream

(photographed above)

Ingredients

4 eggs
½ cup caster sugar
⅓ cup cornflour
3 teaspoons cinnamon
½ cup sugar
½ cup water
½ cup walnuts
1½ cups PURE CREAM (lightly whipped)
icing sugar (for dusting)

Method

1. Beat the eggs and caster sugar together until thick and fluffy. Sift the cornflour and cinnamon onto the surface and fold in lightly.
2. Pour into a buttered and GLAD Bake-lined 28cm x 35cm Swissroll tin and bake (at 200°C) for 15 minutes (or until cooked).
3. Turn out onto a damp tea-towel, remove the paper, and roll up gently lengthways. Allow to cool.
4. Heat the sugar and water in a saucepan, stirring until dissolved. Boil rapidly without stirring (until golden).
5. Dip the walnuts in the toffee and allow to cool on greaseproof paper. Chop roughly and reserve a quarter of a cup. Fold remaining nuts through three quarters of the cream, just before serving.
6. Fill the roulade with the toffeed walnut cream and roll as for a Swiss roll.
7. Dust with icing sugar and decorate with remaining cream and toffeed nuts.

Serves 12

Crème Caramel

Ingredients

Caramel:

¼ cup caster sugar
2 tablespoons water
1 teaspoon lemon juice

Custard:

1¼ cups CREAM
1 teaspoon vanilla essence
3 eggs
1 tablespoon caster sugar

Method

1. Combine caramel ingredients in a microwave-safe jug and microwave on High (100%) for 5 minutes (or until caramel begins to colour). Pour into 6 individual moulds.
2. Combine all custard ingredients and pour into mould. Cook for 4 minutes on MEDIUM/LOW (30%), then allow to stand for 3 minutes.
3. Cook for another 4 minutes on MEDIUM/LOW (30%) and stand for 5 minutes. Invert onto serving dish and serve.

Note: Caramels may also be served chilled.

Serves 6

Jaffa Almond Ring Cake

(photographed below)

Ingredients

3 eggs
1 cup sugar
¾ cup REDUCED CREAM
1⅓ cups self-raising flour
1½ tablespoons Grand Marnier or brandy
2 teaspoons orange rind (grated)
2 tablespoons apricot jam or orange marmalade
2 tablespoons cocoa
¼ cup almonds (slivered)
melted chocolate and almonds (for garnish)
PURE CREAM (lightly whipped, for serving)

Method

1. Beat the eggs and sugar together until light and fluffy. Fold in cream, flour, Grand Marnier and orange rind.
2. Place a quarter of the mixture in a bowl, and mix in the jam, cocoa and almonds.
3. Pour the plain mixture into a buttered 5 cup ring tin, and top with cocoa mixture. Bake (at 180°C) for 50 minutes (or until cooked when tested). Allow to cool on a wire rack.
4. Decorate with melted chocolate and almonds. Fill centre of cake with freshly whipped cream, prior to serving.

Serves 12

Jaffa Almond Ring Cake

Caramel Cream Apple Tarts

(photographed below)

Ingredients

2½ sheets frozen shortcrust pastry (thawed)
1 x 425g can pie apple
1 tablespoon brandy
20g BUTTER
½ cup brown sugar
2 tablespoons water
1¼ cups CRÈME FRAÎCHE
3 eggs (lightly beaten)
extra CRÈME FRAÎCHE (whipped, for serving)

Method

1. Line 8cm x 10cm tartlet tins with pastry. Divide the apple evenly between the tarts, and sprinkle with brandy.
2. Heat the butter, sugar and water, stirring until the sugar dissolves. Boil rapidly for 5 minutes. Allow to cool slightly.
3. Stir in cream and eggs. Pour the custard over the apple. Bake (at 200°C) for 10 minutes, then reduce (to 180°C) for a further 20 minutes (until set). Allow to cool.
4. Serve with whipped crème fraîche.

Serves 6

Chocolate Chip Meringues

Ingredients

125g plain chocolate cake covering
4 egg whites
225g caster sugar
300mL FRESH DOUBLE or WHIPPING CREAM

Method

1. Finely grate the chocolate through a mouli grater.
2. Whisk the egg whites until stiff (but not dry in appearance). Whisk in 4 level teaspoons caster sugar, keeping the mixture stiff. Fold in the remaining sugar with the grated chocolate.
3. Spoon out into 12 meringues onto a GLAD Bake-lined baking sheet, allowing them room to spread.
4. Bake in the oven (at 130°C) for abour 1½ hours (until dry). Peel off the paper and cool on a wire rack. Store an airtight container (if you wish).
5. To serve, whip the fresh cream (until softly stiff) and use to sandwich together the meringues.

Serves 6

Caramel Cream Apple Tarts

Irish Coffee Mousse

Ingredients

2 eggs (separated)
¼ cup caster sugar
¼ cup strong black coffee
2 tablespoons Irish Whiskey
2 teaspoons gelatine (dissolved in 1 tablespoon hot water)
1½ cups PURE CREAM (lightly whipped)
coffee beans (for garnish)

Method

1. Beat the yolks, sugar and coffee together (until thick and creamy). Stir in whiskey and dissolved gelatine.
2. Pour into Irish coffee glasses and refrigerate (until set). Serve garnished with remaining cream and coffee beans.

Serves 6

Weights & Measures

Cooking is not an exact science: one does not require finely calibrated scales, pipettes and scientific equipment to cook, but the conversion to metric measures in some countries, and its interpretation, must have intimidated many a good cook.

Weights are given in the recipes only for ingredients such as meats, fish, poultry and some vegetables. However, a few grams or ounces one way or another will not affect the success of your dish.

Although recipes have been tested using the Australian Standard 250mL cup, 20mL tablespoon and 5mL teaspoon, they will work just as well with the US and Canadian 8 fluid ounce cup, or the UK 300mL cup. We have used graduated cup measures (in preference to tablespoon measures) so that proportions are always the same. Where tablespoon measures have been given, these are not crucial measures, so using the smaller tablespoon of the US or UK will not affect the success of the recipe. At least we all agree on the teaspoon size.

For breads, cakes, pastries, etc., the only area which might cause concern is where eggs are used, as proportions will then vary. If working with a 250mL or 300mL cup, use large eggs (60g or 2 oz), adding a little more liquid to the recipe for 300mL cup measures if it seems necessary. Use the medium-sized eggs (55g or 1¼ oz) with a 8 fl oz cup measure. A graduated set of measuring cups and spoons is recommended, the cups, in particular, being recommended for measuring dry ingredients. Remember to level such ingredients.

ENGLISH AND AMERICAN MEASURES

ENGLISH

All measurements are similar to Australian with two exceptions: (i) the English cup measures 10 fluid ounces (300mL), whereas the Australian cup measures 8 fluid ounces (250mL); and (ii) the English tablespoon (the Australian dessertspoon) measures 14.8mL against the Australian tablespoon of 20mL.

AMERICAN

The American reputed pint is 16 fluid ounces, a quart is equal to 32 fluid ounces, and the American gallon is 128 fluid ounces. The Imperial measurement is 20 fluid ounces to the pint, 40 fluid ounces to the quart, and 160 fluid ounces to one gallon. The American tablespoon is equal to 14.8mL, and the teaspoon is 5mL. The cup measure is 8 fluid ounces (250mL), the same as Australia.

DRY MEASURES

All the measures are level, so when you have filled a cup or spoon, level it off with the edge of a knife.

The scale below is the 'cook's equivalent', *and is not an exact conversion of metric to imperial measurement.*

The exact metric equivalent is 2.2046 lb = 1kg
or 1 lb = 0.45359kg

METRIC		IMPERIAL	
g = grams		oz = ounces	
kg = kilograms		lb = pound	
15g		½ oz	
20g		⅔ oz	
30g		1 oz	
60g		2 oz	
90g		3 oz	
125g		4 oz	¼ lb
155g		5 oz	
185g		6 oz	
220g		7 oz	
250g		8 oz	½ lb
280g		9 oz	
315g		10 oz	
345g		11 oz	
375g		12 oz	¾lb
410g		13 oz	
440g		14 oz	
470g		15 oz	
1000g	1kg	35.2 oz	2.2 lb
	1.5kg		3.3 lb

OVEN TEMPERATURES

The Celsius temperatures given here are not exact; they have been rounded off and are given as a guide only. Follow the manufacturer's temperature guide, relating it to oven description given in the recipe. Remember gas ovens are hottest at the top, electric ovens at the bottom and convection fan-forced ovens are usually even throughout. We include Regulo numbers for gas cookers which may assist. To convert °C to °F multiply °C by 9 and divide by 5, then add 32.

	°C	°F	REGULO
Very slow	120	250	1
Slow	150	300	2
Moderately slow	150	325	3
Moderate	180	350	4
Moderately hot	190–200	370–400	5–6
Hot	210–220	410–440	6–7
Very hot	230	450	8
Super hot	250–290	475–500	9–10

CAKE DISH SIZES

METRIC	IMPERIAL
15cm	6"
18cm	7"
20cm	8"
23cm	9"

LOAF DISH SIZES

METRIC	IMPERIAL
23cm x 12cm	9" x 5"
25cm x 8cm	10" x 3"
28cm x 18cm	11" x 7"

LIQUID MEASURES

METRIC mL millilitres	IMPERIAL fl oz fluid ounce	CUP & SPOON
5mL	1/6 fl oz	1 teaspoon
20mL	2/3 fl oz	1 tablespoon
30mL	1 fl oz	1 tablespoon plus 2 teaspoons
60mL	2 fl oz	1/4 cup
85mL	2 1/2 fl oz	1/3 cup
100mL	3 fl oz	3/8 cup
125mL	4 fl oz	1/2 cup
150mL	5 fl oz	1/4 pint, 1 gill
250mL	8 fl oz	1 cup
300mL	10 fl oz	1/2 pint
360mL	12 fl oz	1 1/2 cups
420mL	14 fl oz	1 3/4 cups
500mL	16 fl oz	2 cups
600mL	20 fl oz	1 pint, 2 1/2 cups
1 litre	35 fl oz	1 3/4 pints, 4 cups

CUP MEASUREMENTS

One cup is equal to the following weights.

	METRIC	IMPERIAL
Almonds, flaked	90g	3 oz
Almonds, slivered, ground	125g	4 oz
Almonds, kernels	155g	5 oz
Apples, dried, chopped	125g	4 oz
Apricots, dried, chopped	190g	6 oz
Breadcrumbs, packet	125g	4 oz
Breadcumbs, soft	60g	2 oz
Cheese, grated	125g	4 oz
Choc Bits	155g	5 oz
Coconut, desiccated	90g	3 oz
Cornflakes	30g	1 oz
Currants	155g	5 oz
Flour	125g	4 oz
Fruit, dried (mixed, sultanas etc.)	185g	6 oz
Ginger, crystallised, glacé	250g	8 oz
Honey, treacle, golden syrup	315g	10 oz
Mixed Peel	220g	7 oz
Nuts, chopped	125g	4 oz
Prunes, chopped	220g	7 oz
Rice, cooked	155g	5 oz
Rice, uncooked	185g	6 oz
Rolled Oats	90g	3 oz
Sesame Seeds	125g	4 oz
Shortening (butter, margarine)	250g	8 oz
Sugar, brown	155g	5 oz
Sugar, granulated or caster	250g	8 oz
Sugar, sifted icing	155g	5 oz
Wheat germ	60g	2 oz

LENGTH

Some of us are still having trouble converting imperial to metric. In this scale measures have been rounded off to the easiest-to-use and most acceptable figures.

To obtain the exact metric equivalent to convert inches to centimetres, multiply inches by 2.54

Therefore 1 inch equals 25.4 millimetres and 1 millimetre equals 0.03937 inches

METRIC mm = millimetres cm = centimetres	IMPERIAL in = inches ft = feet
5mm (0.5cm)	1/4 in
10mm (1.0cm)	1/2 in
20mm (2.0cm)	3/4 in
25mm (2.5cm)	1 in
50mm (5cm)	2 in
80mm (8cm)	3 in
100mm (10cm)	4 in
120mm (12cm)	5 in
150mm (15cm)	6 in
180mm (18cm)	7 in
200mm (20cm)	8 in
230mm (23cm)	9 in
250mm (25cm)	10 in
280mm (28cm)	11 in
300mm (30cm)	1 ft (12 in)

Glossary

acidulated water: water with added acid, such as lemon juice or vinegar, which prevents discolouration of ingredients, particularly fruit or vegetables; the proportion of acid to water is 1 teaspoon per 300mL

al dente: Italian cooking term for ingredients that are cooked until tender but still firm to the bite; usually applied to pasta

americaine: method of serving seafood—usually lobster and monkfish—in a sauce flavoured with olive oil, aromatic herbs, tomatoes, white wine, fish stock, brandy and tarragon

an glaise: cooking style for simple cooked dishes such as boiled vegetables; assiette an glaise is a plate of cold cooked meats

antipasto: Italian for 'before the meal'; it denotes an assortment of cold meats,vegetables and cheeses, often marinated, served as an hors d'œuvre; a typical antipasto might include salami, prosciutto, marinated artichoke hearts, anchovy fillets, olives, tuna fish and Provolone cheese

au gratin: food sprinkled with breadcrumbs, often covered with cheese sauce and browned until a crisp coating forms

balsamic vinegar: a mild, extremely fragrant wine-based vinegar made in northern Italy; traditionally, the vinegar is aged for at least seven years in a series of casks made of various woods

baste: to moisten food while it is cooking by spooning or brushing on liquid or fat

baine marie: a saucepan standing in a large pan which is filled with boiling water to keep liquids at simmering point; a double boiler will do the same job

beat: to stir thoroughly and vigourously

beurre manie: equal quantities of butter and flour kneaded together and added a little at a time to thicken a stew or casserole

bird: *see* **paupiette**

blanc: a cooking liquid made by adding flour and lemon juice to water in order to keep certain vegetables from discolouring as they cook

blanch: to plunge into boiling water and then (in some cases) into coldwater; fruits and nuts are blanched to remove skin easily

blanquette: a white stew of lamb, veal or chicken, bound with egg yolks and cream, and accompanied by onion and mushrooms

blend: to mix thoroughly

bonne femme: dishes cooked in the traditional French 'housewife' style; chicken and pork *bonne femme* are garnished with bacon, potatoes and baby onion; fish *bonne femme* with mushrooms in a white wine sauce

bou guet garni: a bunch of herbs, usually consisting of sprigs of parsley, thyme, marjoram, rosemary, a bayleaf, peppercorns and cloves, tied in muslin and used to flavour stews and casseroles

braise: to cook whole or large pieces of poultry, game, fish, meat or vegetables in a small amount of wine, stock or other liquid in a closed pot; often the main ingredient is first browned in fat and then cooked in a low oven or very slowly on top of the stove; braising suits tough meats and older birds, and produces a mellow, rich sauce

broil: the American term for grilling food

brown: to cook in a small amount of fat until brown

bulgur: a type of cracked wheat in which the kernels are steamed and dried before being cracked

buttered: to spread with softened or melted butter

butterfly: to slit a piece of food in half horizontally, cutting it almost through so that when opened it resembles butterfly wings; chops, large prawns and thick fish fillets are often butterflied so that they cook more quickly

buttermilk: a tangy, low-fat cultured milk product the slight acidity of which makes it an ideal marinade base for poultry

calzone: a semicircular pocket of pizza dough, stuffed with meat or vegetables, sealed and baked

caramelise: to melt sugar until it is a golden brown syrup

champignons: small mushrooms, usually canned

chasseur: (hunter) a French cooking style in which meat and chicken dishes are cooked with mushrooms, shallots, white wine, and often tomato

clarify: to melt butter and drain the oil off the sediment

coat: to cover with a thin layer of flour, sugar, nuts, crumbs, poppy or sesame seeds, cinnamon sugar or a few of the ground spices

concasser: to chop coarsely, usually tomatoes

confit: from the French verb *confire*, meaning to preserve; refers to food that is made into a preserve by cooking very slowly and thoroughly until tender; in the case of meat (such as duck or goose) it is cooked in its own fat, and covered with it, so that it does not come into contact with the air; vegetables such as onions are good in *confit*

consommé: a clear soup usually made from beef

coulis: a thin purée, usually of fresh or cooked fruit or vegetables, which is soft enough to pour (*couler* means to run); a coulis may be rough-textured or very smooth

court bouillon: the liquid in which fish, poultry or meat is cooked; it usually consists of water with bayleaf, onion, carrots and salt (and freshly ground black pepper to taste); other additives can include wine, vinegar, stock, garlic or spring onions (scallions)

couscous: cereal processed from semolina into pellets, traditionally steamed and served with meat and vegetables in the classic North African stew of the same name

cruciferous vegetables: certain members of the mustard, cabbage and turnip families with cross-shaped flowers and strong aromas and flavours

cream: to make soft, smooth and creamy by rubbing with back of spoon or by beating with mixer; usually applied to fat and sugar

croûtons: small toasted or fried cubes of bread

crudites: raw vegetables, whether cutin slices or sticks, to nibble plain or with a dipping sauce, or shredded and tossed as salad with a simple dressing

cube: to cut into small pieces with 6 equal sides

curdle: to cause milk or sauce to separate into solid and liquid (for example, overcooked egg mixtures)

daikon radish: (also called mooli): a long white Japanese radish

dark sesame oil: (also called Oriental sesame oil): dark polyunsaturated oil with a low burning point, used for seasoning; (do not replace with lighter sesame oil)

deglaze: to dissolve congealed cooking juices or glaze on the bottom of a pan by adding a liquid, then scraping and stirring vigourously whilst bringing the liquid to the boil; juices may be used to make gravy or to add to sauce

degrease: to skim grease from the surface of liquid; if possible the liquid should be chilled so the fat solidifies; if not, skim off most of the fat with a large metal spoon, then trail strips of paper towel on the surface of the liquid to remove any remaining globules

devilled: a dish or sauce that is highly seasoned with a hot ingredient such as mustard, Worcestershire sauce or cayenne pepper

dice: to cut into small cubes

dietary-fibre: a plant-cell material that is undigested or only partially digested in the human body, but which promotes healthy digestion of other food matter

dissolve: mix a dry ingredient with liquid until absorbed

dredge: to coat with a dry ingredient, such as flour or sugar

drizzle: to pour in a fine thread-like stream over a surface

dust: to sprinkle or coat lightly with flour or icing sugar

Dutch oven: a heavy casserole with a lid, usually made from cast iron or pottery

emulsion: a mixture of two liquids that are not mutually soluble—for example, oil and water

entrée: in Europe, the 'entry' or hors d'œuvre; in North America entrée means the main course

fillet: special cut of beef, lamb, pork or veal; breast of poultry and game; fish cut off the bone lengthways

flake: to break into small pieces with a fork

flame: to ignite warmed alcohol over food

fold-in: a gentle, careful combining of a light or delicate mixture with a heavier mixture using a metal spoon

fricassee: a dish in which poultry, fish or vegetables are bound together with a white or veloute sauce; in Britain and the United States, the name applies to an old-fashioned dish of chicken in a creamy sauce

galette: sweet or savoury mixture shaped as a flat round

garnish: to decorate food, usually with something edible

gastrique: caramelised sugar deglazed with vinegar and used in fruit-flavoured savoury sauces, in such dishes as duck with orange

glaze: a thin coating of beaten egg, syrup or aspic which is brushed over pastry, fruits or cooked meats
gluten: a protein in flour that is developed when dough is kneaded, making it elastic
gratin: a dish cooked in the oven or under the grill so that it develops a brown crust; bread crumbs or cheese may be sprinkled on top first; shallow gratin dishes ensure a maximum area of crust
grease: to rub or brush lightly with oil or fat
joint: to cut poultry, game or small animals into serving pieces by dividing at the joint
julienne: to cut food into match-like strips
knead: to work dough using the heel of the hand with a pressing motion, while stretching and folding the dough
line: to cover the inside of a container with paper, to protect or aid in removing mixture
infuse: to immerse herbs, spices or other flavourings in hot liquid to flavour it; infusion takes from 2–5 minutes depending on the flavouring; the liquid should be very hot but not boiling
jardiniere: a garnish of garden vegetables, typically carrots, pickling onions, French beans and turnips
lights: lungs of an animal, used in various meat preparations such as pâtès and faggots
macerate: to soak food in liquid to soften
marinade: a seasoned liquid, usually an oil and acid mixture, in which meats or other foods are soaked to soften and give more flavour
marinara: Italian 'sailor's style' cooking that does not apply to any particular combination of ingredients; marinara tomato sauce for pasta is most familiar
marinate: to let food stand in a marinade to season and tenderise
mask: to cover cooked food with sauce
melt: to heat until liquified
mince: to grind into very small pieces
mix: to combine ingredients by stirring
monounsaturated fats: one of three types of fats found in foods; are believed not to raise the level of cholesterol in the blood
niçoise: a garnish of tomatoes, garlic and black olives; a salad with anchovy, tuna and French beans is typical
non-reactive pan: a cooking pan the surface of which does not chemically react with food; materials used include stainless steel, enamel, glass and some alloys
noisette: small 'nut' of lamb cut from boned loin or rack that is rolled, tied and cut in neat slices; noisette also means flavoured with hazel nuts, or butter cooked to a nut brown colour
normande: a cooking style for fish, with a garnish of shrimp, mussels and mushrooms in a white wine cream sauce; for poultry and meat, a sauce with cream, Calvados and apple
olive oil: various grades of oil extract from olives; extra virgin olive oil has a full, fruity flavour and the lowest acidity; virgin olive oil is slightly higher in acidity and lighter in flavour; pure olive oil is a processed blend of olive oils and has the highest acidity and lightest taste
panade: a mixture for binding stuffings and dumplings, notably *quenelles*, often of choux pastry or simply bread crumbs; a *panade* may also be made of *fran gipane*, puréed potatoes or rice
papillote: to cook food in oiled or buttered greasepoof paper or aluminium foil; also a decorative frill to cover bone ends of chops and poultry drumsticks
parboil: to boil or simmer until part-cooked (that is, cooked further than when blanching)
pare: to cut away outside covering
pâtè: a paste of meat or seafood used as a spread for toast or crackers
paupiette: a thin slice of meat, poultry or fish spread with a savoury stuffing and rolled; in the United States this is also called 'bird' and in Britain an 'olive'
peel: to strip away outside covering
plump: to soak in liquid or moisten thoroughly until full and round
poach: to simmer gently in enough hot liquid to cover, using care to retain shape of food
polyunsaturated fat: one of the three types of fats found in food; these exist in large quantities in such vegetable oils as safflower, sunflower, corn and soyabean; these fats lower the level of cholesterol in the blood
purée: a smooth paste, usually of vegetables or fruits, made by putting foods through a sieve, food mill or liquefying in a blender or food processor
ragout: traditionally a well-seasoned, rich stew containing meat, vegetables and wine; nowadays, a term applied to any stewed mixture
ramekins: small oval or round individual baking dishes
reconstitute: to put moisture back into dehydrated foods by soaking in liquid
reduce: to cook over a very high heat, uncovered, until the liquid is reduced by evaporation
refresh: to cool hot food quickly, either under running water or by plunging it into iced water, to stop it cooking; particularly for vegetables and occasionally for shellfish
rice vinegar: mild, fragrant vinegar that is less sweet than cider vinegar and not as harsh as distilled malt vinegar; Japanese rice vinegar is milder than the Chinese variety
roulade: a piece of meat, usually pork or veal, that is spread with stuffing, rolled and often braised or poached; a roulade may also be a sweet or savoury mixture that is baked in a Swiss roll tin or paper case, filled with a contrasting filling, and rolled
rubbing-in: a method of incorporating fat into flour, by use of fingertips only; also incorporates air into mixture
safflower oil: the vegetable oil that contains the highest proportion of polyunsaturated fats
salsa: a juice derived from the main ingredient being cooked or a sauce added to a dish to enhance its flavour; in Italy the term is often used for pasta sauces; in Mexico the name usually applies to uncooked sauces served as an accompaniment, especially to corn chips
saturated fats: one of the three types of fats found in foods; these exist in large quantities in animal products, coconut and palm oils; they raise the level of cholesterol in the blood; as high cholesterol levels may cause heart disease, saturated fat consumption is recommended to be less than 15 per cent of kilojoules provided by the daily diet
sauté: to cook or brown in small amount of hot fat
score: to mark food with cuts, notches of lines to prevent curling or to make food more attractive
scald: to bring just to boiling point, usually for milk; also to rinse with boiling water
sear: to brown surface quickly over high heat in hot dish
seasoned flour: flour with salt and pepper added
sift: to shake a dry, powdered substance through a sieve or sifter to remove any lumps and give lightness
simmer: to cook food gently in liquid that bubbles steadily just below boiling point so that the food cooks in even heat without breaking up
singe: to quickly flame poultry to remove all traces of feathers after plucking
skim: to remove a surface layer (often of impurities and scum) from a liquid with a metal spoon or small ladle
slivered: sliced in long, thin pieces; usually refers to nuts, especially almonds
soften: re gelatine—sprinkle over cold water and allow to gel (soften) then dissolve and liquefy
souse: to cover food, particularly fish, in wine vinegar and spices and cook slowly; the food is cooled in the same liquid; sousing gives food a pickled flavour
steep: to soak in warm or cold liquid in order to soften food and draw out strong flavours or impurities
stir-fry: to cook thin slices of meat and vegetable over a high heat in a small amount of oil, stirring constantly to cook evenly in a short time; traditionally cooked in a wok, however a heavy-based frying pan may be used
stock: a liquid containing flavours, extracts and nutrients of bones, meat, fish or vegetables
stud: to adorn with; for example, baked ham studded with whole cloves
sugo: an Italian sauce made from the liquid or juice extracted from fruit or meat during cooking
sweat: to cook sliced or chopped food, usually vegetables, in a little fat and no liquid over very low heat; GLAD-Foil is pressed on top so that the food steams in its own juices, usually before being added to other dishes
timbale: a creamy mixture of vegetables or meat baked in a mould; French for 'kettle-drum'; also denotes a drum-shaped baking dish
thicken: to make a thin, smooth paste by mixing together arrowroot, cornflour or flour with an equal amount of cold water; stir into hot liquid, cook, stirring until thickened
toss: to gently mix ingredients with two forks or fork and spoon
total fat: the individual daily intake of all three fats previously described in this glossary; nutritionists recommend that fats provide no more than 35 per cent of the energy in the diet
vine leaves: tender, lightly flavoured leaves of the grapevine, used in ethnic cuisine as wrappers for savoury mixtures; as the leaves are usually packed in brine, they should be well rinsed before use
whip: to beat rapidly, incorporate air and produce expansion
zest: thin outer layer of citrus fruits containing the aromatic citrus oil; it is usually thinly pared with a vegetable peeler, or grated with a zester or grater to separate it from the bitter white pith underneath

Index

ACKNOWLEDGMENTS

The publishers wish to acknowledge and thank the following companies, corporations and individuals for the supply of products, recipes and props for photography in this book.

The Australian Dairy Corporation especially Marygrace Charlton, Naomi Crisante and Bianca Stafrace for their help and assistance in making this book possible.

The Australian Dairy Corporation for the supply of recipes, photography and data used in this book.

Special acknowledgment to our Consultant Dietitian Carolyn Kelly for her advice and assistance in assembling the manuscript for this book.

NationalPak Pty Limited, for the supply of their marvellous range of GLAD products for use in our test kitchen and photographic studio. The publishers acknowledge that 'GLAD' is a registered trademark of NationalPak Pty Limited.

Jan Wilson for assisting with the testing of numerous recipes in this book and the supply of helpful hints used throughout this book.

The recipes in this book have been compiled by the publisher, and supporting companies do not accept any responsibility for the contents of this book.

MAJOR CREDITS

Published by:
R&R Publishing Pty Ltd
PO Box 1221
Fitzroy North VIC 3068
National Toll-Free:1 800 063 296

Publisher: Richard Carroll
Recipe Development: Australian Dairy Corporation
Co-Ordinator: Marygrace Charlton
Computer Manager: Sean McNamara
Creative Director: Jon Terpstra
Photography: Australian Dairy Corporation
Home Economist: Naomi Crisante (Australian Daily Corp)
Cooking Tips: Jan Wilson
Editor/Proof Reader: Rev. Dr Ross Gilham

The National Library of Australia
Cataloguing-in-Publication Data.
Fresh food cooking with dairyfood.
Includes index.
ISBN: 1 875655 63 8 (pbk)
ISBN: 1875655 62 X (case)
1. Cookery (Dairy products). 2. (Series: Fresh food cooking).
641.67

This edition printed February 1998
Computer typeset in Bookman and Avant garde by:
R&R Publishing Pty Ltd, Fitzroy North, VIC, Australia
Film Scanning: PICA Overseas, Singapore
Printed in Singapore by: Toppan Printing Co.